the spirit of
bonsai design

the spirit of
bonsai design

combine the power
of zen and nature

CHYE TAN

COLLINS & BROWN

First published in Great Britain in 2003
by Collins & Brown Limited
The Chrysalis Building
Bramley Road
London W10 6SP

An imprint of **Chrysalis** Books Group plc

9 8 7 6 5 4 3 2 1

British Library Cataloguing-in-Publication Data: A catalogue
record for this book is available from the British Library.

ISBN: 1-84340-021-9

Designed by Anne Wilson
Edited by Hilary Mandelberg
Indexed by Isobel McLean
Proofread by Sharon Amos

Color reproduction by Classic Scan Pte Ltd
Printed by Times Offset (M) Sdn. Bhd, Malaysia

contents

introduction

The main aim of this book is to introduce bonsai styles evocative of the Zen spirit. The elegant trunks and weeping branches of the willow tree inspire us to craft certain features on a bonsai to evoke the same feelings of enchantment. This bonsai style is known as the Weeping style (see page 78). Another bonsai style which typifies the Zen spirit is the Literati style (see page 84–85). You will discover its intriguing, abstract form and how it came into being.

I have also invented my own bonsai style, which I christened Hobbit style (see page 90–93). It was inspired by the film *The Lord of the Rings*. One dramatic scene made a lasting impression on my bonsai-filled imagination. It showed the enormous, gnarled roots of a giant tree where the hobbits took shelter from their enemies. This powerfully atmospheric feature can be reproduced quite easily on a bonsai and is the basis for my new style.

Most of the bonsai created in this book were inspired by nature. Whenever possible, bonsai growers should imitate only the most beautiful or pleasing features found on natural trees. They must also remember that a bonsai needs care and nurturing. Watering, weeding, fertilizing, pruning and transplanting must all be carried out diligently and at the proper time.

In addition to the basic Japanese methods of training bonsai, I have devised several effective pruning and shaping techniques of my own, which are described in this book. I hope with these to show the difference between achieving a beautiful bonsai and an outstanding one. Step-by-step instructions and photographs show how certain bonsai were created. These are designed to inform and inspire both the novice and the experienced grower.

Beautiful bonsai creations have the power to fill us with joy and satisfaction, but it can take an enormous amount of time and patience to instill those elements of Zen esthetics into the tree to produce the desired effects. Consciously or not, when we look at bonsai, we are drawn towards nature and we experience tranquility that nurtures the mind and spirit. It is a pleasure and a privilege for me to share my experiences and skill with you.

Chye Tan

RIGHT Beautiful autumnal leaves inspire bonsai growers to imitate nature.

gallery of zen bonsai

Today's bonsai offers many different possibilities. First, there is the infinite variety in the way tree trunks grow in nature. Some of these trunk movements have been classified into bonsai styles and every bonsai should reflect one of them. Then there are the many different varieties of trees from all parts of the world that could be trained into bonsai. Temperate species display colorful changes through four seasons, adding even more to the variety. This Gallery of Bonsai Masterpieces represents the uniqueness, diversity and beauty of the trees on our planet.

▶ lion king

style: Slanting style/shakan
height: 22in (55cm)
species: Chinese juniper/*Juniperus chinensis* 'Shimpaku'
origin: Japan
training: 6 years

ZEN QUALITIES
Skeletal remains on the stem and apex of this juniper testify to its struggle for survival. The clasping surface roots resemble the claw of a lion.

◀ enlightenment

style: Formal Upright style/chokkan
height: 40in (100cm)
species: Bo tree/*Ficus religiosa*
origin: Thailand
training: 20 years

ZEN QUALITIES
The sturdy, ribbed trunk is riddled with dimpled depressions and clefts. It displays an imposing grandeur, which signifies righteousness.

▼ thunder clouds

style: Informal Upright style/moyogi

height: 31¹/₂in (78cm)

species: Black pine/*Pinus thunbergiana*

origin: Japan

training: 30 years

ZEN QUALITIES

Its robust, elegant trunk is encrusted with lichen—suggesting durability and timelessness. The trunk movement strikes a finely tuned balance with "clouds" of foliage on its branches.

▶ solace

style: Weeping style/shidare zukuri

height: 30in (75cm)

species: Dwarf false cypress/*Chamaecyparis pisifera* 'Filifera Nana'

origin: Netherlands

training: 10 years

ZEN QUALITIES

The entrancing, drooping foliage of a weeping tree evokes melancholy as well as enchantment.

▼ winter solitude

style: Forest Bonsai/yose ue

height: 25¹/₂in (55cm)

species: Japanese maple/*Acer palmatum*

origin: Japan

training: 15 years

ZEN QUALITIES

Trees of different sizes create the illusion of depth and perspective in a shallow container. The overall impression of this harmonious, unified forest is one of repose and tranquility.

▶ immortal

style: Driftwood style/sharikan

height: 43in (108cm)

species: Japanese yew/*Taxus cuspidata*

origin: South Korea

training: five years

ZEN QUALITIES

This ancient yew transplanted from the wild retains a high degree of naturalness, providing a powerful subject for contemplation and meditation. The stunning contrast between the brilliant bleached white of the trunk and the fresh, vital spring green of the needles brings to mind Zen concepts of rebirth and a life-giving force.

◀ rising phoenix

style: Exposed-Root style/neagari

height: 20in (50cm)

species: Chinese elm/*Zelkova schneideriana*

origin: China

training: 7 years

ZEN QUALITIES
Like a phoenix in flight, these bare, tenacious roots
cling on precariously for survival.

▼ simple harmony

style: Literati style/bunjin gi

height: 29in (73cm)

species: Scots pine/*Pinus sylvestris*

origin: Scotland

training: 8 years

ZEN QUALITIES
Leaning dramatically, the vitality and spirit of this pine face
gales and blizzards with defiance. Heather planted at the
base of the trunk suggests a wild, windswept environment.

◀ cliff hanger

style: Cascade style/kengai

height: 18in (45cm)

species: Mountain pine/*Pinus mugo*

origin: Netherlands

training: 12 years

ZEN QUALITIES

Every winter, packs of snow weigh down the branches of this
mountain pine. Its cascading branches tumble down like a waterfall.

▼ the sanctuary

style: Hollow-Trunk style/saba kan

height: 25¹/₂in (64cm)

species: Field maple/*Acer campestre*

origin: Netherlands

training: 15 years

ZEN QUALITIES

A heavy, hollow trunk is mysterious and indicates the tree's
determination to survive despite all adversities.

▼ tai chi postures

style: Rooted-on-Rock style/ishitsuki

height:16in (40cm)

species: Chinese elm/*Zelkova schneideriana*

origin: China, cuttings

training: seven years

ZEN QUALITIES
The lichen-covered rocks and elegant trunk movements of the elms in this miniature landscape convey the essence of the aesthetic concept of wabi-sabi. The tiny pagoda serves to emphasize the height of the trees, heightening the sense of austere, serene beauty.

▶ dignity

style: Twin-Trunk style/sokan

height: 33in (83cm)

species: Orange jasmine/*Murraya paniculata*

origin: China

training: 15 years

ZEN QUALITIES
The erect, dignified trunks pair up to form an asymmetrical crown signifying unity and harmony in an idealized Zen form. Exposed to sufficient sunlight, this bonsai produces sweet-scented white blossoms and red berries.

◀ fertility

style: Broom style/hokkidachi

height: 18in (40cm)

species: Dwarf pomegranate/*Punica granatum* var *nana*

origin: Spain

training: 20 years

ZEN QUALITIES

With ample sunshine, its scarlet flowers develop into rosy fruits which hang on bare branches in winter—a symbol of fertility in the cycle of re-birth and re-generation.

▼ french ambiance

style: Landscape Bonsai/saikei

height: 6in (15cm)

species: New Zealand tea/*Leptospermum scoparium* (Nanum Group) 'Kiwi'

origin: Belgium

training: 7 years

ZEN QUALITIES

The rich contrasts in this scene—distant, high mountains and trees growing randomly on a slope—are a lively interplay of opposites that recall vivid memories of almond trees in the south of France.

▼ serpent of the mistral

style: Semi-Cascade style/han kengai

height: 16in (40cm)

species: Scots pine/*Pinus sylvestris*

origin: France, cuttings

training: 20 years

ZEN QUALITIES

Arching dramatically as if contorted by gales, this
Scots pine peers into an abyss.

▶ elegant chi

style: Root-Bundle style

height: 27in (67cm)

species: Chinese elm/*Ulmus parvifolia*

origin: China

training: 15 years

ZEN QUALITIES

This Chinese style simulates a ribbed trunk, typical of fig trees,
which produce numerous aerial roots. The bonsai`s elegant
posture is supported by a strong and graceful trunk.

譯

zen

and the

art of

bonsai

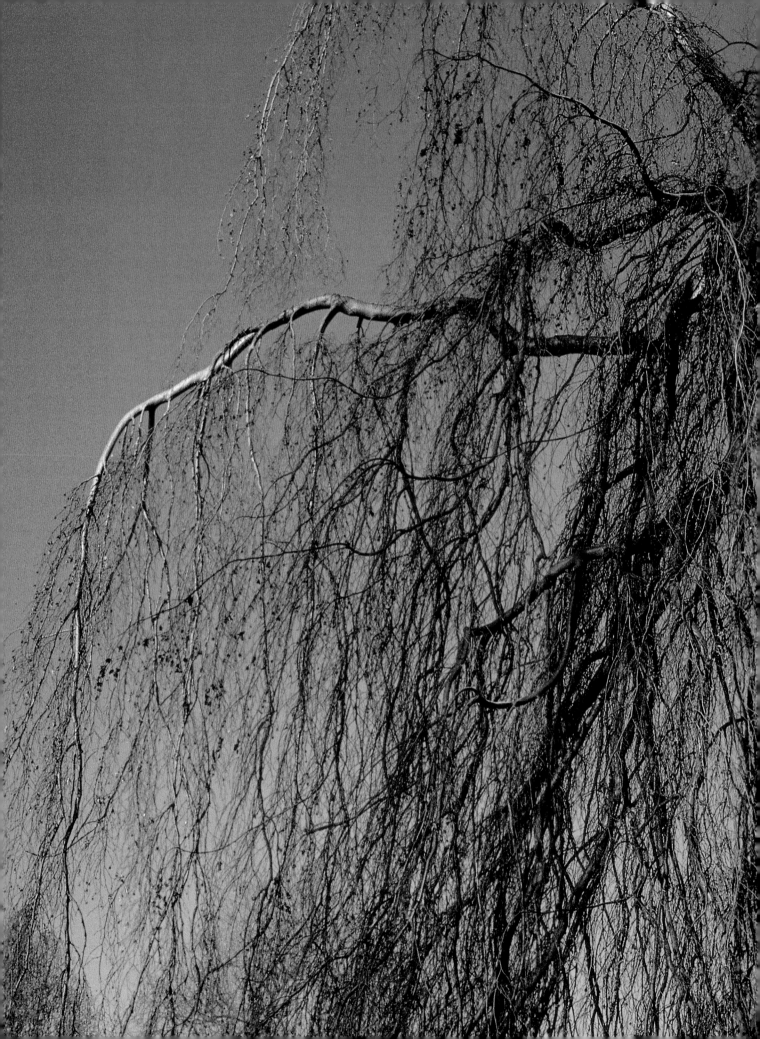

observing
nature

Bonsai growers observe and pick out the most pleasing shapes and structures for the design of the trunk, branches and canopy of a bonsai tree, so you cannot be a bonsai grower without being aware of nature. The majority of us, fortunately, live where we can see trees and shrubs growing. Even in city centers many streets are lined with trees planted to provide shade or for ornament. Then there are the parks and gardens, created for people's enjoyment and carefully planned to anticipate how the fully grown trees would eventually dominate or complement the designed landscape.

With our busy, hurried lifestyles we sometimes forget to pause and contemplate the beauty of these trees. Every type has its distinctive structure and horticultural characteristics, but to be a good observer of nature we have to look beyond the obvious. For example, we can examine the intricate pattern of twigs weeping from the arching branches of a beech. Among the tangle of branches we can notice the angle at which each limb inclines outwards from the trunk (see left) and we can use this observation to help us shape a Weeping style bonsai (see page 86). Or by observing other weeping trees, such as the willow or the weeping ash, we can learn about the subtle differences in trees with this habit.

Those who venture out into wild country, for example to exposed mountain slopes, can study trees that have been stunted and contorted by the effects of wind, snow, or drought. These trees appear different to the same species growing in sheltered lowlands or valleys. The Driftwood style (see page 124) of bonsai can be used to imitate the injuries suffered by these remarkable trees.

In the same way, observation of a mature beech growing in a park shows how it develops a gigantic trunk with robust and firm surface roots (see right). These radiate in all directions—tapering, branching out and creeping into the ground. Only mature, older trees exhibit this tendency so when a bonsai has roots like this, the viewer has the impression of an aged tree, even though the bonsai may be a great deal younger.

The "eye" on a tree trunk testifies to the loss of a branch but

LEFT **Winter exposes the bare branches of a deciduous tree. They radiate energetically outwards, sometimes arching sharply. Secondary branches droop, dangling long tertiary twigs.**

BELOW **Standing majestically on a knoll in the middle of a park, an old beech spreads its enormous root system in all directions.**

sometimes dead branches are still attached to an old tree. The bonsai grower may wish to imitate this, in which case a dead branch, or jin, is left on a bonsai (see page 125). Similarly, in nature, a large branch may be wrenched off a tree by an animal feeding on its foliage and, in the process, a large strip of bark may be torn off the trunk—exposing a lacerated surface. This effect may be imitated on a bonsai by gradually debarking, or removing the bark, from a small area of the trunk, leaving an exposed area known as a shari (see page 125).

the influence of zen

The word Zen means to sit and meditate. Zen Buddhism originated in China as Chan Buddhism, a belief system that borrowed heavily from Taoist philosophy. In this philosophy, Tao is the way in which man should co-exist in harmony with nature. Consequently, Zen Buddhism is not just a religion with many complex doctrines and rituals—it is a way of life.

In the fifteenth and sixteenth centuries, Zen Buddhism reached the peak of its influence in Japan. It had a profound effect on painting, calligraphy, poetry, and the tea ceremony, bringing with it an emphasis on simplicity and austerity, subtlety and tranquility. Garden design, ikebana (the art of flower arrangement) and bonsai also evolved under its influence.

Garden design, which had often been quite ostentatious, became more natural and subdued. Zen gardens (kare-sunsui) were constructed for the sole purpose of meditation. By meditating in front of a rock, a person can understand the essence of the stone, and become one with it. A Zen garden is a landscape in miniature, whose main constituents—rocks, moss, trees, plants, and water—are positioned with enormous attention to detail to evoke various sensations. Gnarled trees and weathered rocks are thoughtfully sited so as to be in harmony with their surroundings, and there is a feeling of balance between Yin and Yang as areas of vegetation are balanced by space or by a body of water. A Zen garden also evokes a feeling of mystery and anticipation: parts of the garden remain hidden as the viewer is confronted with a succession of various scenes. Garden ornaments and flowering plants are few and far between. Stone lanterns and water basins are weathered and covered with moss to blend into the scenery.

Most of these esthetic aspects of Zen Buddhism quickly permeated bonsai design. Just as the Zen ideal of simplicity focuses on the essentials, so by stripping away unnecessary detail, the essence of a bonsai can be better appreciated. Thus by emphasizing tenacious roots or a weathered trunk, the tree's determination to survive in a hostile environment becomes apparent and the bonsai immediately becomes more than just a miniature replica.

Zen esthetics also require that mastery of artistic and technical skills be combined with intuition and sensitivity in order to stimulate the emotional responses of wabi, sabi, shibui, and yugen (see page 36). Just as Taoism emphasizes man's harmony with nature, so the triangular silhouette of a bonsai symbolizes the philosophy of man, earth and heaven in one dynamic harmony.

OPPOSITE This *Taxus baccata* has a dead branch sticking out of the left side of the trunk—known as "jin." The debarked portion of the trunk is known as "shari."

LEFT A partially debarked trunk contrasts the subtle shapes and tones of driftwood areas with the craggy bark.

Zen esthetics emphasize the profound and mysterious. Similarly, Zen esthetics require there to be a sense of balance. In bonsai, asymmetric compositions achieve the desired effect. These and other facets of Zen esthetics are classified under the following headings: economy of expression, simple balanced lines, emotional response, and attention to details.

zen in practice

economy of expression

On a Japanese scroll, sumiye is not a painting in the conventional sense of the word. It is a kind of sketch in black and white, executed with a minimum number of brush strokes, all skillfully controlled by pressure and speed so that different amounts of ink are absorbed by the thin rice paper on which they are painted. The result is varying shades of black left in the lines of the sumi ink (made of soot and glue, and diluted with water).These simple brush strokes can contain a variety of expressions; for example, the swaying of a branch with falling leaves. The scroll painting on the left shows the dramatic trunk movement of a pine leading up to three drooping branches.

This economy of expression, or minimalism, is the basis of bonsai. A bonsai should portray the essence of an immense, mature tree that has been weathered by the elements: wind, snow, or drought. Some branches of a tree struggling in parched terrain will die off due to lack of moisture. Gales will bend trunks and twist sturdy branches. The weight of compacted snow may fracture large branches. Eventually, the tortured tree will develop a gnarled trunk with attractive scars and prominent driftwood.

Such determination to survive against adversity was an inspiration for Zen monks reflecting on life's trials and tribulations. On arduous journeys wandering up mountain paths, pilgrim monks must have observed impressive, ancient trees thriving in harsh conditions. These tenacious trees seemed to possess the power to elevate the spirit and purify the mind. It is not surprising therefore, that the earliest bonsai trees were excavated from the sides of mountains and nurtured in pots by monks.

BELOW Some understanding of calligraphy is essential to the development of minimalist designs in bonsai.

simple, balanced lines

Simple, balanced lines are conveyed in the five basic bonsai styles. Japanese bonsai masters of the last few centuries studied the characteristics of natural trees, in particular the inclination of their trunks, and used their observations to devise the five basic styles (below).

the five basic styles

▦ CHOKKAN OR FORMAL UPRIGHT

Has a perpendicular trunk

▦ MOYOGI OR INFORMAL UPRIGHT

Has a curving trunk with an apex above the trunk base

▦ SHAKAN OR SLANTING

Has a trunk that inclines at an angle of about 45 degrees

▦ HAN-KENGAI OR SEMI-CASCADE

Has a steeply inclined trunk with main branches slanting downwards. They should hang below the level of the surface of the soil but not below the bottom of the pot

▦ KENGAI OR CASCADE

Has a trunk that arches, preferably at a sharp angle, and that grows downwards below the level of the surface of the soil. Its branches can hang below the bottom of the pot

LEFT The graceful, dynamic trunk movements of five basic bonsai styles.

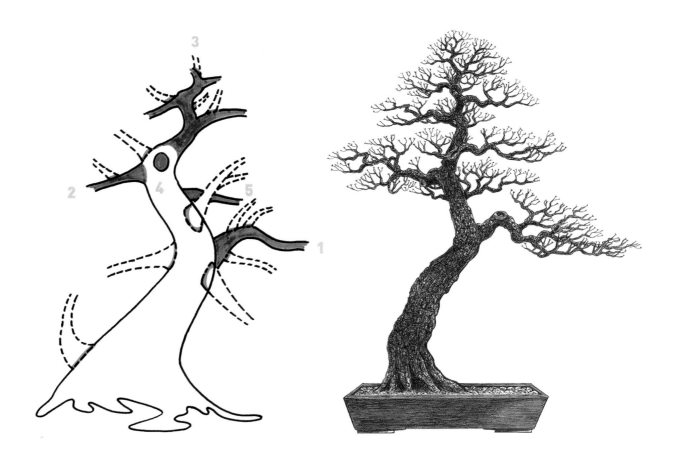

ABOVE LEFT Subtraction method: the principal branches numbers 1, 2 and 3 are marked in green. No. 4 is the "front" branch. No. 5 is the "back" branch.

ABOVE RIGHT Addition method: The principal branches—reduced to simple balanced lines—are allowed to ramify. These new secondary and tertiary branches are added to increase foliage mass in the crown.

Just as an artist sculpting a block of marble must initially chisel off chunks to obtain the rough shape of the sculpture, so a bonsai grower uses the "Subtraction Method" to start to shape a container plant into one of the basic styles. The sketch (above left) shows the principal branches (1, 2, and 3, marked in green). Once these have been located, well-situated complementary branches, including the front and back branches (4 and 5, marked in blue) are retained. All non-essential branches growing in undesirable places (broken lines) should be pruned off (red lines). The retained branches are encouraged to grow secondary and tertiary branches while they undergo periodic pruning and wire shaping. This is known as the "Addition Method." Above right is an artist's impression of how the tree will look after all its branches are fully trained. The lowest branch on the right has been allowed to grow long since mature trees develop heavy lower branches. This lowest branch usually forms the base of a canopy that is asymmetric in shape.

After a thorough study of these styles, a skilful bonsai grower can go on to develop more complicated designs. Depending on how certain branches are manipulated and improvized, unique designs can be created. As a grower gains experience and insight, he will be able to select material that will capture the imagination. Sometimes, the tree itself will suggest a particular design to the artist. This intuitive process is called "listening to the tree."

emotional response

When we were children, many of us had a great deal of fun climbing trees or we may have noticed how one that reached a colossal height could provide cool shade on a warm, sunny day. Decades later, we view these trees with nostalgia. In the same way, we may marvel at the seasonal changes of deciduous trees—the silhouette of branches covered with a splendid canopy of colorful fall leaves, or at the massive girth of a 500-year-old sweet chestnut tree (*Castanea sativa*) that testifies to centuries of hardship and evokes feelings of profound humility.

BELOW LEFT Contrasting with an evergreen pine, the brilliant fall colors of deciduous trees—triggered by cold spells—highlight an exciting seasonal change.

BELOW RIGHT There is a kind of timeless, rugged beauty in the weathered scars of a venerable ancient chestnut tree.

TOP   The desolate abbey ruin and a weeping tree evoke memories of medieval wars and tragedy. Wabi feelings are enhanced by the misty background.

ABOVE   This *Pemphis accidula* with its massive trunk needs a heavy, masculine pot to match its Shibui quality.

Zen art aims to evoke a similar emotional response—the wabi–sabi state of mind—and this is achieved in bonsai through the skilful crafting of horticultural features which produce an emotional response that reverberates in the mind of an observer.

Wabi is associated with feelings of melancholy, nostalgia, loneliness, desolation, austerity, admiration, or adoration. The example on the left shows two trees among the ruins of a cloister, conjuring up an image of desolation. The weeping tree evokes feelings of compassion or sadness. Molds of moss of various textures planted behind the arches suggest a horizon of distant hills that emphasizes the remoteness of this historic site. Weathered rocks beneath the tree are covered with moss and help to enhance the scene's forlorn aspect.

Sabi is associated with feelings of humility, timelessness, ruggedness, remoteness, durability, weathering, earthiness, and restraint. The chestnut tree on page 35 has weathered many storms and witnessed a momentous event. In World War One, soldiers hid in a trench dug next to this tree. It endured countless acts of vandalism and survived a fire. Now towering at more than 80 feet (25m), it is a listed tree, protected by law. Sabi is etched in its rough, wrinkly bark.

Shibui is the impression we get principally from the trunk movement of a bonsai, which may be dynamic, elegant, or majestic, or from the energy in its posture, which may be vigorous, sturdy, lofty, masculine, or feminine. This impression should be taken into account when selecting a container for the bonsai. The example on the left has a powerful trunk that looks undoubtedly masculine, so was planted in a heavy pot. The tree seems to soar majestically into the sky.

Yugen is the mood we experience during the contemplation of a bonsai. In general, most onlookers find beautiful bonsai enchanting and tranquil. However, trees with hollow trunks appear intriguing, and the cavern-like holes formed by exposed roots can seem full of mystery. A split trunk conjures the dramatic image of a tree struck by lightning. An old fig tree draped with aerial roots creates a haunting atmosphere. At the Tagaki Museum in Tokyo, the driftwood stem of one of its oldest juniper trees (right) looks almost mystical.

attention to detail

This is essential if a bonsai is to create the correct impression. To leave some room for the viewer's imagination, some feature or detail may be discreetly added or partially concealed, or a path winding through a forest may disappear behind some bushes. If the woodland is well designed, the viewer will be able to imagine birds singing or the wind whispering. Deep in a forest carpeted with dark green moss, a patch of light green moss will suggest a secret clearing highlighted by sunlight beaming down.

In a similar vein, attention must be paid to the ramification and crown of a bonsai. Fine ramification will make a small bonsai look like a giant tree. The flowering *Leptospermum scoparium* (Nanum Group) 'Kiwi' (below left) is only 6 inches (15cm) tall yet looks like a large tree in miniature. The "cauliflower" crown of a Trident maple (*Acer buergerianum*) shades a massive trunk. On closer examination of the bonsai below right, we can see that the crown is made up of two branches on the left and two on the lower right. There is also a network of secondary branches in the top right portion, all of which demonstrates that attention has been paid to the detailed training to ensure the tree looks natural.

ABOVE Trees with driftwood trunks can be intriguing, dramatic, haunting, awesome, or mystical.

BELOW LEFT The fine ramification in the canopy of a tree establishes perspective by making a small tree appear fairly large.

BELOW RIGHT This concept, known as "hide and reveal" in Zen design, is adopted in the canopy of a Trident maple (*Acer buergerianum*) bonsai. Sections of branch structures are strategically exposed to create distinct layers of foliage in the crown.

design
fundamentals

Training a bonsai combines horticulture, design and shaping. Bonsai growers are inspired by nature as well as by examples of quality bonsai found in books and at shows. Our Japanese predecessors have also left us a wealth of information. They standardized procedures and suggested many important guidelines. A bonsai design consists of the following fundamental parts:

Root formation – stability, impression of age
Trunk lines – taper, movement, weathering
Branch structures and foliage clusters – character, strength
Crown – ramification, mass and space, triangular silhouette
Posture – direction, force, harmony

root formation

One of the most beautiful trees in the collection of a certain bonsai grower in Thailand is a *Ficus religiosa* (left). Its surface roots radiate in all directions into the ground, supporting the giant, flared, base of the trunk. This is known as buttressing. In full-size trees, buttressing prevents a large tree from blowing over in a typhoon. It also provides stability for a tall tree in the jungle competing for sunlight. Cultivating buttressed roots in a bonsai gives an impression of stability that makes the tree look older and more imposing. To encourage buttressing, a mature tree can be planted in shallow soil above a paving stone in the ground for several years.

Although there are various types of root arrangements suited to different styles of bonsai, a Formal Upright or "Broom" style tree should feature well-structured surface roots spreading in all directions from the base of its trunk.

Time and effort must be invested in the cultivation of an impressive root system. This is achieved by meticulous annual root pruning. Once the surface roots have been pruned, the bonsai should be planted in a training pot or in the open ground for several years to allow the feeder roots to develop and the surface roots to thicken. Cover the surface with moss and fertilize the feeder roots, which grow from the thicker roots, with a solution of the rooting compound, Rootone.

OPPOSITE A flared bole strengthens the powerful base of this priceless tropical fig.

LEFT By planting the bonsai on a ceramic slab, the robust spreading roots look more impressive.

Once a good network of feeder roots has developed, the tree can be transplanted into a bonsai pot. The soil should be removed from the mature surface roots and the tree placed on top of a mound of soil so the surface roots are visible above the brim of the pot when the bonsai is viewed at eye-level. Arrange the surface roots into a neat, flowing pattern, with the thicker roots tapering off into a network of thinner roots, similar to the structure of a branch. Roots that are flexible can be separated and twisted into position with your fingers. Those with kinks in should be pegged down with inverted U-shaped wire pins. Fill the rest of the container with soil to just below the brim of the pot.

Bonsai styles were classified by Japanese bonsai masters after long and intensive study of the way in which trees grow in nature. Most styles were defined according to the inclination of the tree trunk. I have selected one prominent style for detailed examination, the Informal Upright or moyogi. Our image of a classical bonsai has always been the pine tree with pronounced bends (see page 42) trained in this style. Its trunk moves in a very dynamic way, twisting, bending, or curving in various directions, and its asymmetric lines are balanced, graceful, and elegant. The traditional rules that define the Informal Upright style help us understand how the various components of the bonsai (branches, trunk, posture, and in most cases the surface roots, are integrated into the overall design.

trunk lines and movement

■ The bottom third of the trunk must not have any branches.

■ The three lowest branches should arise from alternate outer curves in the middle third of the trunk and the back branch must be visible to provide depth to the bonsai.

■ Ideally, the lowest branches should be the biggest in terms of length and thickness. However, in reality, trees seldom branch according to this ideal so compromises have to be made. If the branches are not in the proper locations they may be manipulated by wiring.

■ The top third of the tree should consist of smaller branches that diminish in size as they approach the apex. The apex should be tilted towards the front of the bonsai to give the viewer the illusion that the tree is taller than it actually is.

■ The trunk should taper gradually from base to apex.

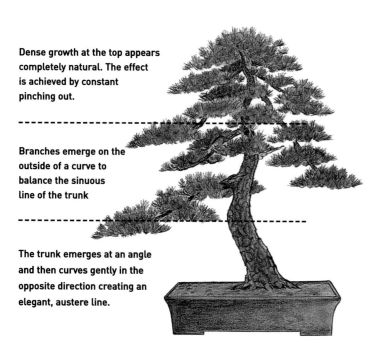

Dense growth at the top appears completely natural. The effect is achieved by constant pinching out.

Branches emerge on the outside of a curve to balance the sinuous line of the trunk

The trunk emerges at an angle and then curves gently in the opposite direction creating an elegant, austere line.

ABOVE One of the most elegant and graceful bonsai styles is the Informal Upright or moyogi. This drawing is an artist's impression of the white pine on page 44.

The central feature of a bonsai is its trunk and different species of tree have different trunk characteristics. For example, a natural smooth-barked species like the Japanese maple should not have any ugly scars and you should take care not to damage the thin bark of an azalea with wires. Pine trees and old broad-leaved trees should have rough bark.

Other characteristics like trunk girth should also be reflected in the bonsai. For instance, an oak tree with a slender trunk would not look as impressive as one with a heavy trunk. By arranging the surface roots of the bonsai radially around the trunk, the trunk will eventually thicken up and flare into the roots. The base of a trunk can also be fattened by encouraging extra branches to grow rampantly around it for several years. Once the trunk is thick enough, these "sacrificial" branches should be completely removed. However, this will leave prominent scars, so these branches should not be allowed to grow at the front of the trunk.

Movement of the trunk along the bottom third is known as tachi-agari in Japanese. In a tree in the Informal Upright style, the line of this part of the trunk is like an elongated "S." This is usually followed by diminishing "S" curves along the middle and top sections of the trunk. These curves may be manipulated by wiring so that the main branches are located at the outer bends on either side of the stem, spiraling all the way to the top of the trunk. The apex itself should consist of numerous twigs growing in all directions (see right).

On some species, the twisted trunk line can be given artificial weathered effects by carving with hand or power tools (see page 124). For example, the trunk of the Chinese juniper is particularly beautiful when a strip of bark is peeled off the stem. The result is known as a shari and will spiral up the trunk, following the curves. Artificial "eyes," or callus collars, clefts, and hollows may also be formed.

Branch structures have to be considered in two parts: the two principal branches and the foliage clusters or pads.

When you start to train a bonsai, you have to first determine which side will be the front. This is the side that shows the best trunk movement relative to the three principal branches—the primary or largest branch (sashi-eda) the counterbalancing branch (uke-eda) and the back branch (sano-eda). The latter is one of the most important complementary branches, providing depth to the bonsai, and so is included in the basic design at this stage. The primary branch should arise from the trunk at about a third to a quarter the height of the tree. This branch establishes the character of the tree, influencing the shape, inclination and emergence of the other branches. Ideally, it should be the lowest branch and should emerge from an outside curve in the trunk. The counterbalancing branch should be on the other side of the trunk from the primary branch. It will be slightly smaller and could be situated higher or lower than the primary branch, but for preference, it should be higher.

Thirdly, since a bonsai is a three-dimensional object, it must have a back branch to provide depth. Whether it is above, below

branch structures & foliage clusters

ABOVE In winter, the dynamic trunk movement and ramification of the branches of a deciduous bonsai are more apparent.

ABOVE The primary or longest branch of a bonsai must be balanced by a less heavy branch on the opposite side of the trunk.

RIGHT A fully trained pine tree that has been completely wire-shaped and repotted into a matching masculine container.

or between the primary and counterbalancing branches, it must be visible from the front of the bonsai.

The branches of a bonsai should, in general, accentuate the movement of the trunk to maintain balance and stability in the tree. If the trunk curves gently, then the branches should do the same, and if the trunk movement is angular and dramatic, then the branches should also bend sharply.

The white pine above left was pruned and wired according to the traditional rules to make an Informal Upright bonsai. To counterbalance the greater visual weight of the primary branch, the counterbalancing branch was inclined steeply and shaped into descending "clouds" of foliage. The back branch apparently did not emerge from behind the trunk, but seemed to lie almost parallel to the primary branch. This fault was camouflaged by a front branch. You should note that it is possible to conceal such faults in evergreen trees, but not in deciduous ones because the faults will be revealed in winter when the tree loses its foliage.

Once the three principal branches of the white pine were selected, side branches alternating from outside curves of the trunk were retained. In general, there should also be front branches beginning above the principal branches. A year later the fully trained white pine was transplanted into a container that accentuated the strong masculine rhythm of its trunk.

Next, the bonsai grower must consider the foliage clusters. There are many different growth patterns for broad-leaved trees as well as for conifers, so this should be done by careful observation of nature and by studying established bonsai masterpieces. The example below left shows how deciduous trees develop the network of branches that carry the foliage clusters. Each main branch of this false acacia (*Robinia pseudoacacia*) divides and subdivides to make a beautiful network of twisted twigs. On the bonsai below right, the

BELOW LEFT One of the most beautiful deciduous trees with branches carrying foliage clusters is the *Robinia pseudoacacia*.

BELOW RIGHT The dense crown of a *Sageretia thea* was clipped into distinct layers of foliage.

ABOVE LEFT Pine trees in nature normally form cloud-like foliage layers.

ABOVE RIGHT Triangular "clouds" of needles on the branches of a conifer form larger triangular profiles, which in turn unite to form an overall asymmetric crown.

network of branches are shaped into layers. A Broom style (see page 57) elm would produce straighter branches and twigs, while the periphery of its crown could be finely ramified into a "cauliflower" profile. Willow trees follow yet another pattern.

Sometimes a broad-leaved bonsai is intentionally developed into the classical Pine Tree style (see page 156), even though this does not reflect its natural growth habit which would be more suited to the Broom style. Conversely, it would be unnatural to cultivate a pine tree in the Broom style, since in nature, a pine tree develops cloud-like layers of foliage (above left). These should be emulated on a pine bonsai. The "cloud" of each secondary branch should be a variation of an asymmetric triangle—distinct or sometimes merging with others. Secondary "clouds" should congregate on a main branch to form a larger asymmetric triangle. The foliage profiles of all the branches of a tree should in turn unite to form an asymmetrically triangular canopy, as illustrated above right.

crown

Constant pinching of the branches on the periphery of a broad-leaved bonsai not only shortens new shoots, but ramifies tertiary branches into twigs. A deciduous tree may also be defoliated (see page 114) to reduce leaf size as well as to encourage ramification. This feature is indispensable as it makes deciduous trees appear large in winter when they are

BELOW **Regular pinching of new growth produces fine, dense twigs. This forest has several domed canopies that have been refined to give an asymmetric profile.**

BOTTOM **This evergreen New Zealand tea (*Leptospermum*) has developed well-structured branches that support a fine tracery of twigs.**

denuded of leaves. The Trident maple (*Acer buergerianum*) forest (above) is an example of this. It looks very impressive thanks to its mass of fine twigs. Its overall triangular silhouette is made up of the rounded tops of several crowns. The crucial balance between mass and space has been achieved by creating some space around the edges as well as under the mass of the crowns.

The crown of a Broom style New Zealand tea (*Leptospermum*) bonsai (bottom right) is more like a dome than a triangle. This emulates nature, where the crown of a very old tree gradually evolves from a rounded-off triangular silhouette into a flattened dome—like that of the gigantic tropical tree pictured above. Although there are some areas without foliage, the canopy of this tree is dense and massive, so the trunk seems small by comparison. On a bonsai a massive canopy should not be balanced by a thin trunk as the bonsai would look too much like an umbrella.

In any bonsai composition the posture of the trunk can convey various impressions—masculinity, femininity, elegance, majesty, robustness, and so on.

The bonsai grower has to be precise about the posture of a particular tree in its pot, otherwise its features will not be

posture

ABOVE In this assembly, each tree was postured according to the movement of other trees in its group. At the same time, the principal branches of every tree had to harmonize with the limbs of other trees within the group.

OPPOSITE ABOVE In this schematic arrangement, the trunk postures of the three trees on the right are infused with more chi, or energy. The other two trunks on the left are much smaller (with less chi) as they are meant to complement the main group in the assembly.

OPPOSITE BELOW On a ramrod-straight trunk, the primary or longest branch on the left enhances the chi on that side, so the tree should be planted a little off-center—to the right of the oval container.

shown to best advantage. The tree should not only sit comfortably at the appropriate spot in the container, but it must be placed correctly in order to display its exact front view. Afterwards, final adjustments of the branches may be made but the perfect posture will ensure:

- that the trunk rises up from the surface of the soil at the correct angle

- the most desirable trunk direction has been achieved

- that the relative directions of the largest branch and the apex are coordinated with respect to the pot and the viewer

- that faults are concealed

- that there is harmony between the direction of trunk and branches or, in a group planting, between all the trees in the group.

If the bonsai container is rectangular or oval, the appropriate spot for the bonsai to be planted is slightly off-center. If the trunk leans towards the right, the tree should be planted more towards the left-hand side of the pot. With an Informal Upright bonsai, the largest branch indicates where the tree should be planted. If it points towards the left, the tree should be positioned more towards the right-hand side of the pot. If the container is round or square, the tree should be in the center.

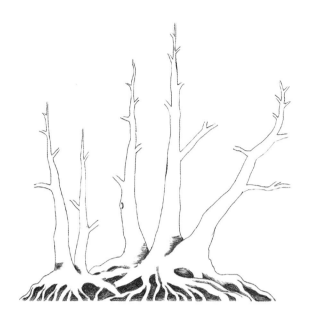

When it comes to group plantings, different rules apply. On page 48 we see five trees divided into two groups. The lines of the trunks of the trees in each group had to harmonize with the others in their group as well as with the trees in the other group. Thus, when the trees were planted, they had to be precisely postured or the composition would not have achieved the desired harmony.

It takes many months or even several years to prepare a tree for competition. Even the slightest change in the direction of a branch could mar the bonsai. Wired branches may be repositioned, but the posture of a trunk cannot be altered unless the bonsai is repotted.

When a ballet dancer is photographed leaping into the air, the resulting image is charged with energy or chi. An experienced sculptor is able to capture that chi in his work. A bonsai artist should aim to do the same and the correct posture of a bonsai in its pot can help to achieve that sense of energy. Tai chi movements often imitate graceful animal postures and these can also inspire bonsai artists to make bonsai with names like Crouching Tiger or Writhing Dragon.

The sketch, top right, shows the direction of five trees. The inclination and direction of each tree is infused with chi, which is enhanced by its posture. If the trunk movements of the five trees did not harmonize and if their directions were not coordinated, they would look lethargic. Without chi the composition would not be lively.

In some instances, it is necessary to wait a long time for a branch to thicken and ramify before chi may be observed in a tree. The Korean beech (right) was heavily pruned to a basic Broom style. Its upper crown (above the second branch) is not in a perfect straight line but the trunk will straighten naturally into the apex after a few growing seasons. When the tree was planted it was positioned slightly to the right-hand side of the pot because its largest branch pointed towards the left. When its branches have ramified into a mass of dense twigs, this 10-year-old beech will look majestic and will exude chi.

starting

from

different

points

three case studies

There are many ways of cultivating and training a tree or shrub into a bonsai. When one is grown from seed, its trunk movement and principal branches can be determined from a very early stage, but its development may take several decades. A less time-consuming method is to select a nursery plant with a thick trunk and ideal branching. A third alternative is to select a partially trained bonsai from a bonsai center and modify and refine it.

the development of a Japanese maple

ORIGIN OF MATERIAL: Seed   TRAINING PERIOD: 20 years

1 Exactly 20 years ago, the author decided to propagate Japanese maples (*Acer palmatum*) from seeds. Only three germinated from a packet of 10 seeds. They grew to a height of around 2 inches (5cm), then two of the saplings died from damping off (see page 156). Unfortunately, there are no photographs of the lone survivor until it was transplanted into a bonsai pot about 10 years later. At that stage, the trunk had too many bends to make it into an Informal Upright style (see page 33), which was what was wanted, so drastic measures were needed. Any very hard pruning of maples should be carried out in winter when the trees are dormant and there is no possibility of bleeding.

2 Firstly. the stem was reduced to the level of the counterbalancing branch on the left. Between the lowest two major branches (right and left) are the front and back branches. Just below the point where the top half of the stem was pruned off, a side branch was wired upwards to form a new apex. This was chosen as the front of the bonsai because of the two major roots radiating from both sides of the base of the trunk.

3 Constant and careful pruning encouraged the apex to branch out, forming new, smaller branches with internodes. Where multiple budding occurred at the internodes, removal of all but two buds prevented the formation of "witch`s brooms" (see page 156). Secondary branches were carefully pruned and wired to develop horizontal foliage clusters. All pruning cuts were made so they would not be visible from the front, otherwise the scars would be seen in winter, and, since a maple bonsai should have unblemished bark, all wires were removed before the branches became marked. In early spring when the buds opened, every new shoot was finger-pinched down to one pair of leaves in order to encourage the growth of tertiary branches, which would then develop fine twigs with diminishing internodes.

4 Two years ago, when the maple was considered fully trained, it was transplanted into a chrysanthemum pot (as shown here), chosen to harmonize with the gentle curves of the Informal Upright style. After transplanting, a kink in the apex was corrected with wiring. Regular soft pruning has produced good ramification and improved tapering in the apex. At the top of the apex, the tapering trunk should divide into dense twigs so that in winter, this ramified canopy gives the viewer the impression of a very large tree.

the re-styling of a Dutch juniper

ORIGIN OF MATERIAL: **Garden center**   TRAINING PERIOD: **10 years**

1 When a painting or piece of sculpture is completed, it cannot be radically altered. Fortunately, in bonsai, it is possible to transform a tree trained in one style into a completely different style. The *Juniperus squamata* 'Meyeri' is a Dutch juniper, a shrub that is widely available at garden centers. It has blue-green needles and a flaky bark. Sometimes an old specimen with a thick trunk can be bought at a reasonable price. A triple-trunk Dutch juniper was selected for a bonsai club evening about 10 years ago. During the two-hour demonstration, one stem was debarked (see page 125) in order to create a double trunk in Mother and Child style (see page 156). The principal branches on the larger trunk were selected to harmonize with the smaller trunk, and the principal branches were wired to lower them . Later, when the partially completed tree was reviewed, the shape of the smaller trunk seemed to detract from the design of the whole bonsai. Its curving trunk was complemented by well-positioned branches, but the larger trunk looked too rigid by comparison.

2 Two years later, and after a great deal of thought, it was decided to convert the larger trunk into driftwood. It was first debarked, then all its secondary branches were wrenched off with jin pliers. The principal branches of the smaller trunk were then allowed to thicken up, while the branches of the apex were constantly pruned to increase ramification.

3 Five years later, the juniper was transplanted into another pot and shaped in Informal Upright style. Heavy wiring and a guy wire were used to create a satisfactory curve on the trunk, but above that, subsequent curves formed a boring zigzag. These ugly curves were corrected at a later stage. Meanwhile, two other problems had to be addressed: The lower trunk was too straight and the principal branches were too thin, but it was too soon to take action.

4 Three years later, all the principal branches had thickened up enough to warrant a final shaping. To change the rigid trunk posture, the trunk was tilted to the left by propping it up temporarily in another pot. This transformed the tree from Informal Upright style into Slanting style. In this style the longest branch should be on the leaning side of the trunk and should be balanced by another principal branch higher up on the opposite side. In this case, that meant the lowest branch on the right had to be eliminated. After wiring and shaping the whole tree, the juniper was finally transplanted into an oval brown pot.

the redesigning of an imported bonsai

ORIGIN OF MATERIAL: **Bonsai center**

TRAINING PERIOD: **five years**

1 The Chinese elm (*Ulmus parvifolia*) is deciduous and should be cultivated outdoors. It should not be confused with *Zelkova schneideriana*, which is evergreen, comes from tropical China and, in temperate climates, should be cultivated indoors. Although it was not fully trained, this Chinese elm was selected from hundreds of other trees because it had a large trunk base and interesting bark. As this species ages, portions of bark flake off to reveal light-brown patches—similar to the bark of a mature plane tree.

2 First, three years of growth in the crown were necessary to increase its size so that it was in proportion to the height and thickness of the trunk. The tree also had an enormous distracting surface root growing diagonally towards the back that needed to be shortened. The tree was also too tall in comparison to the size of its stem, so it was decided to enhance the base of the trunk by reducing its height.

3 After three years, the tree was assessed to determine the level to which its apex could be lowered. Just below this point there needed to be a front branch with numerous side branches to replace the apex. This shows the pruning cut at the back where the apex was removed.

4 By adopting the Zen ideal of using simple balanced lines (see page 33), the elm was reduced to three principal Broom style branches, complemented by smaller front and back branches. Several of these were shaped using wire. The fault in the tree's surface roots was corrected when the elm was transplanted into an oval glazed pot.

5 Subsequent pinching of the peripheral branches encouraged the development of fine twigs and completed the redesign of this imported bonsai.

bonsai styles

rock plantings

On rocky terrain, as long as it can obtain adequate moisture, a tree can grow to its full size. In Qui Lin, China, limestone spires are luxuriantly covered in small trees (below). Trees growing on rocks reflect their tough environment. Their trunks are twisted by gales, their gnarled roots are exposed by erosion. These contorted forms are beautifully depicted in the landscape paintings of Literati painters in China and Japan and are a constant source of inspiration for bonsai artists. Study of the paintings offers many ideas regarding the shaping of a tree, its planting angle, and the selection of a suitable rock to harmonize with the shape of that tree. In America, landscape painters of the Hudson School have produced many fine works of art that can also provide inspiration.

root-over-rock style or seki joju

BELOW A deciduous tree manages to grow on a limestone rock in the midst of rice fields. This spectacular scene can be recreated in a rock planting.

This is a bonsai whose roots embrace a rock, then grow down into the soil of the container, tapering and branching out before they enter the soil. Ideally, a bonsai should have surface roots

that radiate out in all directions, but if you have a tree with thick roots growing unevenly at the base of its trunk, this can be compensated for by planting the tree on a rock. In this way the attention is drawn to the powerful roots gripping the solid structure (top right). The attractive characteristics of the rock also contribute to the beauty of the bonsai.

THE TREE

For a seki joju, the tree is usually selected first. A neglected, pot-bound, container-grown plant should be avoided as its roots cannot be disentangled without endangering the tree. However, most garden center trees are planted deeply in their containers, so get permission to dig into the soil to inspect the roots and study the tree carefully before buying it.

During transplanting, all the soil is removed and the root structure can be examined properly. The tree requires a number of long thick roots that grow, for preference, horizontally out from the base of the trunk. If there is a taproot, it will prevent the tree from sitting comfortably on the rock, while flexible roots have the potential of gripping the rock snugly so there are no gaps between the roots and the surface of the rock. The example, middle right, shows how the roots of the tropical plant *Feroniella lucida* were attached to its rock with long strips of bicycle-tyre rubber. Unfortunately, a wire was later fastened over the roots to force them to grow on the rock, a practice that is not advised as it can mark the roots. While the roots were being trained, the rock planting was retained in a temporary white plastic container on top of a bonsai pot (below right). This retaining pot was filled with very porous soil to keep the roots moist and cylindrical sections of the pot were cut off once a month so that small amounts of soil could be removed bit by bit. The exposed roots gradually became woody, a process that

ABOVE RIGHT Tapering roots clasping a rock seem like streams flowing down a cliff.

CENTER RIGHT The roots of` *Feroniella lucida* have been trained to slither down the clefts of a rock.

BELOW RIGHT The long roots of this rock-clasping bonsai are gradually exposed by cutting off bands of the plastic retaining pot, level by level.

emulates the effects of natural erosion. The roots lower down in the soil needed to lengthen and produce feeder roots to sustain the tree. To encourage this, a fertilizer rich in potassium and phosphorus was put on the surface of the bonsai pot (not on the soil of the plastic retaining pot).

THE ROCK

The next step is the search for a suitable rock. Esthetically it must match the tree, and accommodate the base of the trunk and its roots comfortably. Preference should be given to a sober-colored rock with a rough surface. Its front surface should be eroded with small gullies, interesting holes and indentations (see below). When an eroded surface is covered with a patina of lichen or moss, it possesses an esthetic quality known in Japanese as gei. These beautiful features should be displayed as prominently as possible.

The shape of the rock must harmonize with the style of the tree, so roundish or squareish shapes should be avoided. Other factors which must be considered are the actual spot on the rock where the tree is to be planted, the fissures and chasms where the major roots will grow down the rock, and the height of the rock above the surface of the bonsai tray when the tree is fully trained.

BELOW An assortment of granite rocks with highly eroded surfaces. Asymmetrically shaped rocks with fissures allow roots to cling on and thicken.

Another important factor to remember is that the size of the rock cannot change, even though the tree will continue to grow. Hence, the final shape of the tree must be envisaged in relation to the rock. Trident maples (*Acer buergerianum*) and figs need special care as their roots have a tendency to flatten and broaden on rock surfaces that are warmed up by the sun. If their roots lie too close to each other, they can fuse into a solid mass. If the rock on which they grow is too small or too low, the coalesced roots might, after several decades, completely cover the rock. Care also needs to be taken as powerful roots can easily split soft rocks like coral, sandstone or pumice. And bear in mind that a tree with a rock simply placed next to or in front of it is not a seki joju.

ESTHETIC CONSIDERATIONS

The height of a tree and its rock should not be the same. Tall, slender trees will appear more majestic standing on a low, horizontal rock and will look more esthetically pleasing if planted on one side of the rock. A Cascade style tree (see page 33) often has a short trunk: Planting it high up on a tall rock will evoke its normal habitat—perched on a cliff.

The direction in which tree and rock face must also be carefully considered. In the top illustration, tree and rock both face the same way, or co-ordinate. In the one below, they face in opposite directions, but the tree is still in harmony with its rock. There is a vital difference between the two rock plantings. In the first case, the roots grow naturally down the rock. This approach would not seem natural in the second example, so the roots have been hidden behind the rocks. Strictly speaking, the second example is not considered to be a seki joju.

Besides moss and miniature grasses, a rock-grown bonsai can be beautified by the addition of tiny accent plants like sedum, cotoneaster, myrtle, or thyme.

THE PRACTICALITIES OF SEKI JOJU

Sometimes a rock has to be positioned at a certain angle in the soil, but it should be properly supported so that the bonsai looks stable. The tree must also look as if it is growing naturally

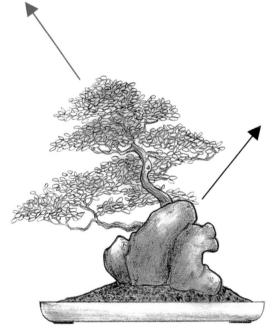

TOP Although the directions of both tree and rock are similar, the rock planting looks harmonious.

ABOVE The direction of the rock and that of the tree, although opposing, are orchestrated to complement each other. These opposing characteristics give rise to a highly dynamic composition. However, this rock-grown bonsai cannot be considered as a Root-over-Rock style because no roots are visible to the viewer.

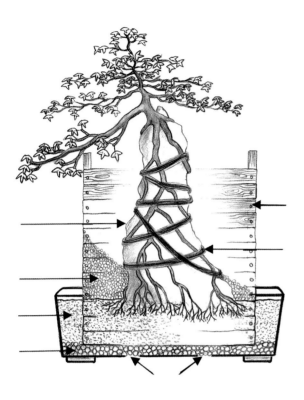

ABOVE A training box constructed of panels. The removal of each panel from top to bottom simulates the erosion of the soil surrounding the elongated roots clasping their rock. When the thick roots are exposed they lignify.

on the rock, so you need to observe nature and study landscape scroll paintings.

The best binding materials to attach the tree to the rock in the initial stages are raffia or cotton cloth such as gauze bandage. Raffia is a natural material that will start to decay after a year in moist conditions. If you use plastic raffia, watch out for scarring as this type of raffia does not decay. An improvized piece of rubber (such as used inside a bicycle tyre) is indestructible and expands as the roots thicken.

To encourage roots to cling to their rock and not produce feeder roots, the rock planting should be surrounded by very porous soil. If you can obtain the Japanese volcanic soil, Akadama (see page 156), it should be mixed with an equal portion of sieved granite chips of similar grain size. (If this isn't available use pumice.) Instead of a plastic container, plastic netting can be used as a retainer or, for very tall rock plantings, a wooden box made of panels can be used (see left). The panels can be taken off, a level at a time, so the soil can be removed and the roots gradually exposed.

In seki joju style, the rock itself can occupy quite a lot of space in the bonsai tray and the roots may fill the remaining space much sooner than expected, so repot in good time. Always make sure that the drainage is exceptionally good, using a layer of granite chips to prevent the drainage holes from clogging up. After transplanting, water the bonsai with a solution of 2 teaspoons (10ml) vitamin B1 dissolved in 2 pints (1 litre) of water. This will assist the recovery of stressed roots.

The tray should be as shallow as possible (without compromising the drainage). This gives the viewer the impression that both tree and rock are taller than they actually are ... illusions of grandeur.

400 years at Angkor

One of the world's most impressive archaeological sites lies deep in the jungle of Cambodia at Angkor. This was the center of the Khmer empire between the ninth and the fifteenth centuries, and during that period, many temples and monuments were built there. After a third catastrophic invasion from neighbouring Siam in 1431, the Khmer civilisation started to decline and Angkor was abandoned. Over the course of 400 years, the voracious jungle almost completely smothered the ancient capital. The mighty roots of trees gripped the masonry like the claws of monsters.

Many of the beautiful temples at Angkor were damaged by weather and by the roots of the trees, but ironically, this endowed the ruins with a timeless, haunting Zen quality that fills visitors to Angkor with awe. Angkor offers bonsai growers the challenge of recreating a fragment of the ruins with miniature trees, and allows enthusiasts to combine fantasy and reality in a very personal way.

PREPARATION

With the right materials, the task of portraying a giant tree growing on the ruins at Angkor can be accomplished in a surprisingly short time. The author managed to find a bas-relief of a Buddha, similar to the one decorating the ruined gate tower (below, right), in an aquarium shop. As the ceramic ornament was matt-glazed, it acquired a patina after a few years in a moist environment.

The rock required was very special as it had to incorporate the ceramic ornament as well as allow the tree's roots to grow over the bas-relief. Finally, a rock was discovered with a shoulder-like protrusion , reminiscent of the Buddha tower. The rock had to be modified using a hammer, chisel, and drill in order for the main roots of the bonsai to grow over it, then the ornament was cemented on in such a way as to allow the roots to clamber over the bas-relief (see page 66, top). This determined the front of the rock. After the cement had completely dried, the rock was soaked in water to leech out any harmful chemical elements until it was ready for use.

A Chinese elm with a slender trunk and branching similar to that of trees in a jungle had been growing unsuccessfully on a rock for several years. Its roots were not clasping the rock properly so it was chosen for the new rock planting. With very few exceptions, an established rock planting should never be extricated from its rock as its roots will be severely damaged.

BELOW Trees grow rapidly in the warm and humid atmosphere of a tropical jungle. Rampant roots are capable of enveloping ancient wall carvings.

BOTTOM Serpentine roots grip masonry like the claws of a monster.

65

TOP **In an exceptional case, an ornament was discreetly cemented to a rock to give the appearance of sinuous roots snaking down an ancient façade.**

ABOVE **The root display of the elm on its previous rock left a lot to be desired. It was planted too low, so not much of its root system was shown to advantage.**

OPPOSITE **At Angkor, the enormous roots of a giant tree grasp an ancient monument in a timeless, mystical setting.**

This tree possessed serpentine roots. Carefully, and with a lot of patience, the elm was detached from its rock so there was minimal damage to its massive root structure. After studying the root system, a tentative front was decided on in conjuction with its new rock. The tree was moved into a temporary pot filled with very porous soil to await transfer to its next home. To minimize stress, trees for rock planting should be root-pruned as little as possible and the sandy soil mixture (three parts sharp sand to one part potting soil) should be checked regularly to make sure the roots are always moist.

PLANTING PROCEDURE

As soon as new buds appeared on the elm, the rock was smeared with a thick layer of keto (see page 156) and the crevices were filled with some more. The tree was wired and lightly pruned, then it was carefully removed from its training pot and the roots exposed. Taking care to keep it facing the right way, the tree was maneuvered into position on the shoulder of the rock. Its main roots were positioned in the clefts in the rock and others were positioned over the bas-relief so as not to obscure the face of the Buddha. A layer of keto was plastered over the exposed roots and raffia was then repeatedly wrapped over these roots to bind them snugly, but not too tightly, onto the rock. The keto was covered with moss and kept constantly moist by spraying with water at least once a day.

The rock planting was then lowered into a training pot filled with porous soil. Its branches were wired and lowered since drooping branches make a tree look older. This is a radical departure from the structure of a jungle tree, which usually has upward-growing branches, but the bonsai would not have appeared harmonious if a young-looking tree had been planted on an ancient-looking monument. Sometimes compromises have to be made to add to the illusion.

After thorough watering, the rock planting was left in a greenhouse for three weeks and its soil checked daily to ensure it did not dry out. After three weeks, the rock planting was moved out of the greenhouse and placed in a shaded area protected from the wind. After about six months, the raffia was cut off and some of the keto was eroded artificially by slowly and

carefully squirting jets of water onto its surface. Once the keto was washed off, the roots would lignify over the bas-relief.

Normally, it takes between one and two years for roots to clasp a rock, but in this case, the roots had already been growing over a similar-shaped rock, so they clung on after six months. Without disturbing the rootball, the rock and elm were carefully moved into a specially made bonsai tray. The main focus of this bonsai is its sinuous roots—a reminder of those trees that grew rampantly for 400 years at Angkor.

waterfall elms

The successful production of a bonsai depends on the availability of suitable material and its adaptability in a composition. To recreate something of the scenery shown below, a group of multi-trunked elms (*Ulmus minor*) was selected to dominate this seki joju. They possessed exposed roots that evoked the eroding force of a gushing river. In the real landscape, the river is not very obvious and the birch trees in the center of

BELOW A cascading stream makes a "U-" turn around a group of birch trees. This feature was adopted to include a clump of elms growing on a rock.

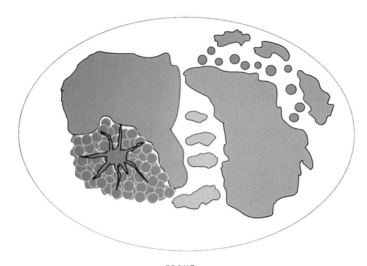

FRONT

LEFT Top view of the positions of the promontory
and waterfall rocks, together with the elm trees and
a distant forest of junipers.

BELOW More than a decade ago, the multi-trunk
elms below were part of a group planting.

the photograph look quite insignificant. Nevertheless, the
photograph provided inspiration.

Suitable rocks were found to suggest the waterfall and to
provide a promontory to which the elms could cling. One other
important component in the landscape was a Raft style (see
page 156) Chinese juniper. When planted to represent a distant
forest, it added depth to the scene. The illustration above is a
schematic drawing of all the components of this seki joju.

In order to accommodate the large rocks, a huge 2-foot (60cm)
long tray was chosen and its drainage holes were covered with
plastic netting. The tray was filled with granite chips to promote
better drainage, followed by a layer of bonsai soil (two-thirds
potting soil and a third of coarse, sharp sand).

Fourteen years ago, the multi-trunked elms formed part of
a bonsai in the Group Planting style (above right). They were
separated from the rest of the group because they had
developed long, claw-like roots, an ideal feature for a rock
planting. After selecting their front, the elm trees were wired up
and their trunk movements shaped to harmonize with one
another. The roots of the elms were fastened to the promontory
of the large rock with keto and raffia. The rock was positioned
in the tray, slightly off-center. With its steep side on the left, the
long rock was positioned on an incline to the right of the large rock
to enable a waterfall to be built between them. The long rock was

propped up at its raised end with stones, and white gravel was channeled into the space between the two rocks. Tiny stones were placed in the path of the cascading water and shell grit was carefully scattered on top of the gravel to imitate falling water.

The Raft style Chinese juniper (below) was planted behind the waterfall, on top of a hill so that its branches emerged like a forest in the distance. Moss was used to cover all the keto and tiny plants were inserted into the crevices in the rocks. The immense landscape composed simply of two groups of trees and several rocks stirs the imagination—giving an overall impression of unity, repose, and tranquility, evocative of the Zen spirit.

BELOW **A scene recreated with a Root-over-Rock style clump of elms and a Raft style Chinese juniper.**

rock-grown style or ishitsuki

In an ishitsuki rock planting, the rootball is contained on or in the rock. This style is sometimes known as the Rooted-on-a-Rock style. The growth of the rootball is restricted in the cavity and root pruning is rarely possible. If the rootball is clinging to the surface of an indentation or to a ledge, it can broaden out slightly and tiny sections of overgrown root can be sliced off and fresh keto introduced into the rootball to rejuvenate the tree. Pellets of slow-release fertilizer can also be inserted into the keto. However a tree growing in the crevice of an actual rock will eventually degenerate when its roots have no more room to expand. The only solution seems to be to plant the whole ishitsuki in the ground, or in a huge pot, with the soil level completely covering the rootball. After a few years the tree will put out new roots that will grow outside the rock cavity. When these roots are long and thick enough, they can be trained to grow down the rock as a seki joju.

Compared to seki joju, the surface roots of an ishitsuki are seldom displayed. It is the rock that dominates the design. An ishitsuki can suggest a distant landscape. Above, a small tree grows on a rock at a beach resort in Spain. This scene is the sort that could be etched in the memory of a bonsai lover and used as the inspiration for a nostalgic ishitsuki.

ko tapoo

From the beginning of the Ming dynasty (1368) to the end of the Ching dynasty (1911), the imperial court in Beijing would leave the Forbidden City to escape the stifling summer heat. The royal family would take up residence at their summer palace, surrounded by beautiful lakes and gardens. Some of the buildings are connected by covered walkways whose eaves are decorated with Literati paintings (see page 60) of scenery from other parts of China. One of these paintings features a rock outcrop topped with pine trees, soaring out of a valley (below).

Similar examples of this type of spectacular scenery can be found in the south of Thailand. Near the coral island of Ko Phi Phi, a limestone rock has been eroded to such an extent that its base has become shaped like the neck of a bottle. This unique 230 foot (70m) high rock is called Ko Tapoo, meaning "nail island." It is so small that it can only support small trees and thickets (opposite, left). The gigantic rock soars out of the ocean with enormous chi. Erect but storm-blasted, it epitomizes the Zen qualities of resilience, perseverance and timelessness.

This famous rock is known to many bonsai lovers in Thailand but no one had ever attempted to create a Ko Tapoo bonsai. Out of the blue, a Ko Tapoo look-alike rock from Thailand appeared at a bonsai center in the Netherlands. The author immediately recognized the shape and was thrilled to purchase it. This amazing rock is only 30 inches (75cm) tall, but weighs over 110 pounds (50kg) (opposite, right). It was skillfully constructed from smaller, columnar pieces of slate. The grain and strata of every piece ran vertically, and their surfaces were covered with a gorgeous patina. Overhanging projections resembled stalactites.

To make the bonsai, every aspect of this many-faceted rock was carefully studied so that its front could be determined. Three cavities of various sizes were found at the top and their relative positions, as well as the best rock face, were the deciding factors.

BELOW A Literati landscape adorns the eaves of a walkway at the summer palace near Beijing in China. In the middle of the painting is a craggy rock topped with pine trees.

LEFT Near Ko Phi Phi in south Thailand, the famous rock, Ko Tapoo, soars spectacularly out of the ocean.

ABOVE An enterprising stone craftsman constructed a replica of Ko Tapoo from separate pieces of Thai slate. It was then exported to the Netherlands.

Various landscape compositions were possible, but certain esthetic aspects had to be considered too. Imitating the greenery that actually grows on Ko Tapoo would not have made an interesting bonsai. If pine trees similar to those depicted in the Literati painting had been used, they would have been out of proportion, unless dwarf spruces were used. If the trees were very small and of a species with tiny leaves or needles, the rock would look taller. The success of the final composition would depend on the number of trees used, their position in relation to each other and to the rock, and their styles of growth.

In the final analysis, use the plant material that is available. Fully trained mame bonsai (see page 156) are very expensive, while garden center plants may have large rootballs that have to be reduced in stages, probably during the course of two pruning seasons. Fortunately, the author had begun the

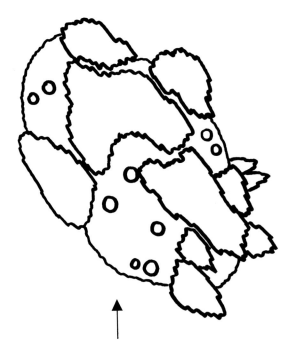

ABOVE **Top view of the rock showing the planting areas for groups of Chinese junipers.**

OPPOSITE **Without attempting to create an exact copy of the natural scene, storm-battered junipers flourish on top of a fantastic rock.**

training of some Raft style Chinese junipers about five years previously. Separate trees, 4–6 inches (10–15cm) tall, had been created from the branches of a parent plant. One of these trees was divided in two by pruning. Each section had enough roots to sustain it.

A first group of five trees was planted in the largest cavity in the foreground (see left). The second group consisted of three shorter trees. These were wired and planted in the medium-sized cavity on the left, at the back. The tree on the extreme left of this group was bent into a Semi-Cascade (see page 33). The third group on the right-hand side of the example opposite was made up of two juniper cuttings. These exceptionally small trees look as if they are growing on a distant precipice. They add depth to the composition. Ko Tapoo now rises out of a 40 by 80-inch (1 x 2.1m) bed of gravel, next to the author's conservatory.

phuket chasm

Off the coast of Phuket in Thailand there is a rocky island with a chasm running right through its base. This fantastic geological feature provided the inspiration for the bonsai on page 76 (left). An assortment of Thai slate was used to make the rock, with the different pieces joined together with colored cement. To make the rock look convincing, all the separate pieces were chosen to match one another in strata, grain, color, and texture. A creeping juniper (*Juniperus prostrata*) fitted comfortably on top of the rock, which had an opening (the chasm) under its right side. The tree was then left to recuperate for a year.

When it was time to style the tree, the front of the rock had to be determined. The juniper was completely wired and shaped into a windswept Semi-Cascade (see page 33), with a sweeping back branch to provide depth to the planting (page 76, right), and with sedum inserted into the crevice. Special attention was needed for the areas where the rocks were joined since, even though colored cement had been used, some of the joints were very obvious. They were concealed with clay and planted over with moss and creepers.

When a photograph of the rock planting was studied, the tree did not quite harmonize with its rock. The rock looked too

ABOVE A tall rock with an overhang was specially constructed for a prostrate juniper. The most beautiful, or front, view of the rock was selected to highlight a chasm running through its base.

OPPOSITE With the addition of a pinnacle, the rock seemed less rectangular in shape. The cascading branches of the juniper were diverted toward the right and across the entrance to the cave. Both tree and rock are in harmony.

rectangular, so to soften the effect and create the illusion that the juniper was growing more towards the right, a tower made from two specially selected stalagmite-like rocks was erected next to the tree, and stalagmite-like rocks were added to the chasm to emphasize its cave-like qualities.

Then the longest branch of the juniper was brought over to the right to shade the chasm entrance, and its foliage was shaped into "clouds." The apex of the tree was slightly lower than the highest part of the rock (opposite). As an alternative approach it could have been higher, but whatever the choice, the two elements should never be the same height. Creeping baby's tears (*Soleirolia soleirolii*) was planted just above the chasm entrance so it would hang down, and tiny fern-like *Cotula potentilloides* and other accent plants were planted on top of the chasm to evoke the sort of vegetation that is found near caves. When they dangle over the entrance of the caves they accentuate the Zen mystery in the chasm.

forest bonsai

Tropical forests everywhere are being chopped down at an alarming rate for commercial exploitation. Besides upsetting the ecological system and endangering rare species of plants and animals, the demise of trees reduces the earth's capacity for "breathing." In Cambodia, the Forestry Department has a poster with a poignant message: Love and protect the forest. Perhaps if more bonsai growers were encouraged to create and display forest bonsai, it would increase public awareness of the need for forest conservation.

Where there are national parks to enjoy, nature ramblers have the chance to admire exceptional forest panoramas. The rest of us must resort to public parks and gardens with forested areas. For example, one section of London's Hyde Park was planted with trees that conformed to the notion of a forest (below). The biggest trees are in the foreground, medium-sized trees stand behind them, and smaller trees are at the back and sides of the group. The planting has depth and perspective and the group has an overall triangular silhouette. These elements largely coincide with the principles of Forest Bonsai planting, formulated by the Japanese bonsai masters of the past. They are the features we have to observe when we look to trees and landscapes for inspiration.

BELOW The most pleasing profile for a distant forest is an asymmetric one. Taller trees are in front and smaller trees behind and at the sides.

The best time to view the structure of deciduous trees in a forest is in winter. Below, mixed broad-leaved trees of various ages and of different structural characteristics have been grown together for many years. The whole has a triangular silhouette and looks harmonious, while the hanging creepers in this haunting-looking forest enhance its sense of desolation—a Zen ethestic aspect that could be recreated in a bonsai.

CHOOSING THE SPECIES OF TREES

Depending on the height of the forest we wish to create, we should choose a species with tiny leaves or short needles, and with small flowers and fruits. One species worthy of mention is the edible pomegranate (*Punica granatum*). Its apple-like fruit comes in various sizes, but these are too large for a Forest Bonsai unless the forest is taller than 20 inches (50cm). However, the dwarf pomegranate *Punica granatum* var *nana* produces inedible fruits the size of marbles, and their leaves are smaller in proportion. In addition, while some varieties of the edible pomegranate must be at least 10 years old before they fruit, dwarf varieties can fruit when they are only one year old. The branch structure of the dwarf pomegranate is much finer too, and this is an important feature of a Forest Bonsai. *Punica granatum* var *nana* is recommended for its lovely

BELOW In winter, the eerie silhouette of bare trees can be studied.

changing seasonal display. Its leaves turn golden in the fall and it has tiny rosy fruits hanging on bare branches in winter. In late summer, the flowers sprout like orange-red shooting stars.

One species that can rival the dwarf pomegranate is the larch. It is one of very few conifers that are deciduous, with its needles turning golden-yellow in the fall. It also has beautiful, tiny pink flowers, but they often go unnoticed as they usually grow quite high up the tree. On a bonsai, we can watch their green fruits ripen rapidly into the gorgeous brown cones that decorate the bare branches in winter for many years. In addition, as the trees mature, their bark acquires a rugged texture.

The European larch, (*Larix decidua*), is an easy species to work with. It branches profusely, has relatively short needles, and buds from old wood. The trunks of young larch trees can easily be shaped by wiring. Saplings can be found in some forests, but young trees are often available at garden centers. Choose one- to four-year-old specimens growing in small pots. Sometimes a bundle of 50 bare-rooted saplings of various sizes can be bought cheaply.

PLANTING LAYOUTS

In the construction of a forest bonsai, the method based on creating asymmetric triangles with trees of different sizes at each corner seems to produce the best esthetic results. The plan below shows numbered circles representing the cross-

RIGHT **A plan view of the forest with circles representing cross-sections of trees. Trees A, B and C were positioned at the apices of an obtuse triangle. The numbered (smaller) trees were grouped with the major trees following a triangular planting principle.**

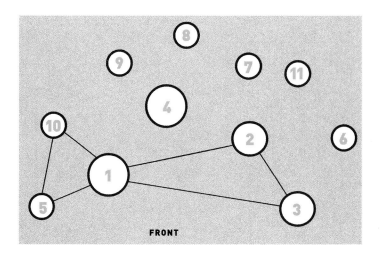

FRONT

sections of the trees. The three largest trees in the forest are A, B and C. A is taller and thicker than B and C is shorter and thinner than B. These trees are laid out as an asymmetric triangle together with smaller trees that have numbers assigned to them. The ascending numbers denote trees of diminishing sizes. Thus tree number 1 is taller and thicker than number 2, number 3 is shorter and thinner than number 2, and so on.

The main trees A, B and C form the largest obtuse triangle in the forest. It is imperative not to plant the tallest tree, A, in the center of the bonsai pot as it will give a more pleasing asymmetric silhouette if it is off-center. When the assembly is viewed from the front, every tree trunk must be visible. The Zen concept of portraying more with less makes the forest look dense without being overcrowded.

THE TREES

For the best esthetic effect, a forest bonsai should always contain more than seven trees. Obtain more than you need so you can set some aside for future expansion of the forest, or to replace dead trees. They should be of various heights and thicknesses. In this example, 20 larch trees were purchased, but only 13 were used. Line the trees up according to size, and number them (right).

THE POT

The size of the pot will depend on the number of trees and the eventual height of the forest. Its long side should either be about a third longer or a third shorter than the height of the tallest tree. If it is shorter, the forest will look tall and compact and if it is longer, more space can be incorporated in and around the forest in specific areas, making the setting look more like a forested landscape.

In most instances, a forest should first be planted in a training pot and transplanted after two years. This is for a number of reasons. First, the rootballs of most trees must be reduced gradually to enable the trees to be planted close together. Second, it may not be possible to shorten the taproot of a tree to the right length at the initial transplanting as this will result in a shortage of feeder roots. It may have to wait until a second

BELOW One- to three-year-old larch trees were numbered according to size. The bonsai pot, fitted with wires, contained a layer of granite chips for drainage.

ABOVE Topping off reduces the height of a tree to a level where a side branch could be wired upward to form its new apex.

BELOW The three major trees A, B, and C were secured by garden wires in their respective positions.

transplanting. Third, roots will recover better after severe pruning if they are in a bigger, deeper pot with better draining soil. Conifer forests should be planted in unglazed brown or gray pots, while broad-leaved trees can be in glazed, colored pots.

THE SOIL

A free-draining mixture is required, consisting of two-thirds of sharp sand and one third of potting soil, or equal parts of sharp sand, potting soil and decomposed larch-needle litter. Place a thin layer of this soil on top of the drainage layer in the training pot.

the potted forest

This larch forest was planted in spring, the best time to plant as the buds are swelling. First the front of each of the main trees was determined. The tallest trees in any forest always lose their lower branches, so the lower branches of trees A, B, and C were pruned off. Tree A, being the most dominant, needed to have mature branches at a level higher than the tops of its subsidiary trees, 1 and 2. Fortunately, these branches could be created by topping-off (as shown left). Just below that, a side branch with very good branching was wired upwards to form the crown.

The trees were removed from their pots and the rootballs loosened. As much soil as possible was shaken off, then the thick roots were pruned off and the rootballs reduced. Each tree was studied carefully, turning it around until the best branching could be seen from its front. Trees A, B and C were positioned to form the asymmetric triangle and some moist soil was put around the rootballs to stabilize their trunks (below).

The smaller trees 1 and 2 were selected and partnered with tree A to form an asymmetric triangle. This was repeated with the rest of the smaller trees. Care was taken to ensure that their branches complemented each other and they were planted behind the larger trees to create perspective. Observation of nature shows that succeeding generations of smaller, younger trees naturally grow at the periphery of a forest (opposite, top).

A well-designed forest bonsai should also incorporate some empty space, more on one side of the forest than on the other.

This balancing of mass with space—yin with yang—emphasizes the profile of the forest. There should also be some space at the front. This space is an important feature of a forested landscape as it entices birds to fly into the forest. Finally, the trees behind the forest should not be planted right up to the edge of the pot. Room must be left for the roots to grow.

Once the trees were all planted, more soil was carefully worked in around the roots with a chopstick, and the rootballs were secured by wrapping gardening wires around them. The soil was topped up, and the surface dressed with a layer of moss (right).

As soon as the planting was complete, the pot was stood in a tub of water, making sure that the water level came just below the rim of the pot. It was removed after about 20 minutes and placed out of the sun and wind, and in a frost-free place. It was misted with water several times a day, but not watered until the soil was almost dry. As soon as there was new growth (after two to three weeks) the forest was gradually moved to a position where it would receive full sun. When it dried out too quickly, it was moved to a place where there was less sun and wind. Below you can see the potted forest four weeks after it was planted.

TRAINING

To start with, only a few of the trees were wired since at this stage it is not necessary to pay attention to detailed shaping. They were allowed to grow secondary and tertiary branches then, when the next repotting was due, the branches were wired and lowered, in late autumn and winter. The wires were checked occasionally and removed as soon as there were any signs of scarring.

ABOVE RIGHT Small trees 1 and 2, and 3 and 4 were grouped round tree A. Smaller trees 5 and 6 were grouped with tree B.

CENTER RIGHT Minor trees 7 and 8, and 9 and 10 were grouped with tree C and tree 6 respectively. Another three reserved trees were added to the right side of the forest.

BELOW RIGHT One month later, the potted forest put out a flush of new needles.

During the growing season, all the long shoots were shortened to restrict their growth to the triangular outline of each tree as well as to the triangular silhouette of the whole forest. Superfluous buds and shoots were removed immediately, the growth of horizontal shoots was promoted and strong shoots growing vertically were removed. Branches growing towards the inside of the forest were also removed and the tops of the trees were pruned frequently to prevent the development of coarse, heavy branches. Branches at the periphery of the tree's crown should be twiggy and a tree will look older if its lower branches are longer and thicker.

stone hut in the forest

The European larch (*Larix decidua*) normally grows on the higher slopes of the Alps. It would be wonderful to create an alpine scene in miniature, but the size of the larch needles would be too big in proportion to the tiny trees. However, European larch trees can be used to create a forest of between 8 and 20 inches (20–50cm) tall, when the needles will be in proportion to the height of the trees.

The larch forest (below left) was created with 15 trees following the same planting theory as the potted forest. For the first three years, it was given only basic training. The plan was to refine the individual trees as they got older, but the largest tree looked too

BELOW LEFT The dominant tree in this dense forest seems somewhat too large.

BELOW RIGHT Using the same triangular planting principle, the larch forest was combined with the potted forest in a huge tray 43 inches (110cm) long. A stone hut was discreetly sited in the middle of the forest to amplify the height of the trees.

tall for the assembly so it was decided that it would be better to combine these trees with the potted forest on page 82 in one huge tray 43 inches (110 cm) long. The whole ambitious undertaking was carried out in five hours, including the lowering of branches by wiring.

The forest was planted in two groups. The group on the right had more trees, but the left-hand group had taller trees. The forest floor was then covered with moss to make the setting look lush and serene—and thus instilled with Zen characteristics. Finally, one tree in the middle of the group on the right was pruned off at its base to allow a stone hut to be placed discreetly in the forest (opposite, right).

aged forest

Compared to a plantation of trees of the same age, an old forest consists of trees of different ages, with succeeding generations growing in ever-increasing circles. The forest bonsai shown below is made up of dwarf pomegranate trees (*Punica granatum* var *nana*), dominated by one huge, aged tree. The dwarf pomegranate is semi-tropical, so this forest floor has been covered with the semi-tropical creeping plant, *Soleirolia soleirolii*. If not regularly pruned, this groundcover will become more like woodland undergrowth, providing hiding places for the inhabitants of the forest.

LEFT An ancient pomegranate forest created with trees of varying ages. The trees appear larger when an ornamental animal on the same scale is added.

weeping style bonsai, or shidare zukuri

One of the most graceful trees in any park or garden must be the weeping willow. It is often planted next to a pond or stream and as the tree grows, sunlight reflecting from the surface of the water appears to entice it over the water's edge, its drooping branches almost touching the water. A fully grown willow needs a lot of space: if left unpruned it can reach a height of 50 feet (15m). Willows planted in small gardens are constantly hacked back to control their rapid growth, but unless they are correctly pruned in winter by an experienced gardener, their graceful structure can be ruined.

RIGHT **A properly pruned giant weeping willow with enchanting, dangling foliage.**

A vigorous 30-feet (9m) tall *Salix babylonica* (opposite) was planted alongside the entrance of a large house. Its long, cascading branches sway and rustle in the wind.

Although it is very easy to root a willow from a large branch, not many fine examples of Weeping style bonsai have been created. This is because every winter all the strong branches produced that year must be completely removed, which often results in a pollarded tree with no fine branching. The delicate, elegant silhouette of a mature weeping willow cannot be maintained.

The Weeping style is defined by the drooping or hanging branches of the tree. Bonsai with bunches of hanging flowers, such as wisteria or laburnum are excluded because their branches do not droop. Weeping style bonsai should also have rough bark and hanging clusters of foliage. Unlike a full-size weeping willow, which has a dense crown in summer, a weeping bonsai needs space among its branches.

The trunk of a Weeping style bonsai should preferably be in the Informal Upright style, the Slanting style, or the Semi-Cascading style. Drooping branches look more beautiful on a curving or slanting trunk than on a vertical trunk. Enchanting arching branches weeping from an elegant trunk create an enhancing Zen quality.

SUBSTITUTE SPECIES

Most bonsai growers are unaware of the many species of trees and shrubs that can be used for the weeping style. The *Tsuga canadensis* "Pendula" is a graceful hemlock with drooping, feathery leaves. It grows slowly to a height of 40 inches (102cm) and in fall has tiny brown cones that hang from the ends of its branches. The semi-tropical Australian species, *Leptospernum brachyandrum*, has many characteristics that make it suitable for the Weeping style. It produces plumes of tiny pink flowers on pendulous branches and its rough brown bark contrasts well with its delicate needle-like leaves.

Weeping beech trees are good examples to study, but are rarely made into weeping bonsai because their coarse structure is difficult to train into the delicate shapes that are necessary.

ABOVE **An adult *Leptospermum brachyandrum* reaches a height of nearly 10 feet (3m) at the Singapore Botanic Gardens. Its delicate arching branches have tiny leaves—an ideal Weeping style characteristic.**

The weeping ash, *Fraxinus excelsior* "Pendula" develops an enchanting shape in around 20–30 years. Its crooked trunk and arched branches may be imitated by *Cotoneaster apiculatus* or *C. horizontalis*.

chamaecyparis

Not many species of willow have leaves that can be reduced in size by bonsai techniques. The alternative is to use a tiny-leafed species with branches that can be shaped into arches. An unlikely source is a member of the conifer family, the slow-growing false cypress *Chamaecyparis pisifera* "Filifera Nana," featured as the weeping tree in Medieval Desolation (below left). It has drooping scale-like foliage and can reach a maximum height of 6 feet (1.8m). This 38-inch-tall (97cm) specimen is about 30 years old. As the crown of the tree becomes heavier, the interior branches turn brown due to lack of light. To prevent branches from dying back prematurely, the tree should be thinned regularly.

ABOVE LEFT **After reducing the height of this false cypress, principal branches were selected according to the Informal Upright style. They were then wire-shaped into arches.**

RIGHT **Contrary to the norm, the drooping foliage of a conifer (*Chamaecyparis pisifera* "Filifera Nana") is surprisingly well suited to the Weeping style.**

Several years later, the height of the tree was reduced by jinning (see page 125) the crown right down to its lowest branch on the right. The tree was then reversed back to front, and the main branches were wired and re-positioned. Other selected branches in the crown were wired and shaped to harmonize with an upper stem in Informal Upright style (opposite left). During the next two years, foliage was reduced on the top of the crown while the lower branches were allowed to proliferate.

juniperus oxycedrus

When the author was collecting junipers in a limestone district in the south of France he noticed a difference in the growth habit of some of the *Juniperus oxycedrus*. Most produced compact, rigid foliage but there were some trees with trailing branches that must have been the result of a natural mutation. He decided to collect one of them.

After excavating the tree, the rootball was carefully wrapped in sphagnum moss and burlap cloth. Many of the roots were shortened dramatically and the crown was pruned immediately in order to reduce evaporation of water from the tree. When the author arrived home, the tree was carefully transferred into a plastic training pot and left in a greenhouse to recuperate.

Five years later the juniper was styled into a Weeping style tree. The front was selected to display a fissure that ran along the lower trunk (above right). Unfortunately, the two lowest branches emerged from almost the same level on the trunk and this defect could not be remedied because removal of either branch would result in an unbalanced crown. Above these two branches, the trunk rose vertically. An attempt was made with heavy wiring to bend this rigid section of the trunk to the right-hand side of the tree, but it was unsuccessful.

A further nine years later the bonsai was re-styled and turned back to front. Its height was reduced and every branch in the crown was wired and shaped into the Weeping style (right). This reversal draws the attention of the viewer towards the crown rather than, as previously, towards the trunk. From the new front view, the two lowest branches appear to grow out of the trunk at different levels and other branches seem to spring out

BELOW Another conifer, the *Juniperus oxycedrus*, has a naturally occurring variety with drooping foliage. The old tree was excavated from a windswept mountainside in the south of France. A fissure in the trunk emphasized the tree's struggle for survival, but this front view revealed a flaw in the branching. The two lower branches seemed to emerge from the trunk at the same level.

BOTTOM When the tree was reversed back to front, the two lower branches seemed to grow at different levels. Back-budding produced new shoots that had to be wired into arches.

ABOVE **Stumps of** *Tamarix chinensis* **could be easily rooted and transplanted into a bonsai pot. This well-tapered tree could be developed into an excellent shidare zukuri.**

OPPOSITE **Driftwood was sculpted on a** *Tamarix juniperiana* **but the most important feature of the Weeping style is its arched branches.**

of the slanting trunk like fireworks falling out of the sky. This effect is one of the enchanting features of a shidare zukuri.

tamarisk

One of the most frequently encountered species in the Weeping style is the tamarisk. Old stumps of *Tamarix chinensis* with their fissured bark can easily be rooted for bonsai. Its plume-like foliage is produced in spring. New shoots emerging from undesirable spots should be removed promptly, while hard pruning is usually done in the fall. The example on the left features a beautiful clefted *Tamarix chinensis* trunk with a good, tapered line. Once the feathery leaves have fallen, all the branches should be shaped with wire. Wiring should start from the beginning of each primary branch, and should shape the secondary branches into graceful half-circles. The tertiary branches should be allowed to hang almost vertically. The ends of each branch should be pruned off, leaving an upper, secondary, branch that tapers to the end.

The two European tamarisk varieties that are normally found at garden centers are the *Tamarix tetrandra* and the *Tamarix pentandra*. The former produces light pink flowers, the latter reddish blooms. Although tamarisks are hardy when planted in the garden, bonsai trees need protection from frost. They can be brought out of winter protection in spring and this is the best time to transplant them. If they are not kept moist during the growing season, they will lose branches, even if the soil dries out for only a short period. A well-draining soil will require frequent watering and extra fertilizer.

In Japan, another species, *Tamarix juniperiana*, is often used to create Weeping style bonsai. This has clusters of tiny pink flowers that burst open in summer. When new shoots appear in spring, tertiary branches are selected and shaped by wiring, and undesirable shoots are removed. Hard pruning should be done in winter. Some of the pre-trained tamarisk imported from Japan were layered from old trees. An example can be seen on the page opposite. Here, part of the trunk that was lacking live bark was carved into driftwood, or shari miki, to imitate weather-beaten trees (see page 124).

the challenge of the literati style or bunjin-gi

During the Sung dynasty in China, landscape paintings by scholars of Confucianism, philosophy and the arts—the Literati, or men of letters—often depicted tempest-gnarled trees growing on mountainous terrain. These rugged trees had very few branches, and those they had were usually growing at the apex of a long, slender trunk. The Literati were naturally attracted to bonsai trees that were similar to those they had painted, so bonsai shaped in this style came to be known as Literati style bonsai. In Japan, Literati style bonsai were eagerly sought after by the educated élite, or bunjin, during the Edo period (1600–1868), hence in Japan, Literati style bonsai were referred to as bunjin-gi.

The bunjin were impressed by the tenacity and endurance of trees that survived hostile environments. These extraordinary trees were believed to reflect the stresses and strains of mortal life. Stripped to its bare essentials, a Literati style bonsai also epitomizes the Zen ideals of austerity, simplicity, and subtlety. Most bonsai growers find bunjin-gi exceptionally challenging to design.

BELOW Struggling pines develop slender, crooked trunks with sparse foliage.

Growers who intend to shape trees into bunjin-gi favor trees with contorted trunks collected from nature, usually in

mountainous regions, since the inherent beauty of these specimens cannot easily be replicated by artificial techniques. The dynamic movement of the trunk is fundamental to the design of a Literati style bonsai. The example opposite shows slender trunks curving elegantly up to a crown of small, sparse branches. The pine tree (right), on the other hand, has sharp bends in its trunk, culminating in an apex that splits into two major branches. This captivating feature is one element that may be used in a Literati design.

The Literati style is unique because the conventional rules followed in the shaping of an ordinary bonsai cannot be properly applied to a tree with very few branches and a long, slender trunk. Any branches that cannot complement the movement of the trunk are shortened and fashioned into small jins (see page 125). Sharis or Driftwood (see page 124), can accentuate the movement of the trunk, but a rugged bark without scarring is preferred. Back branches are unnecessary. In some instances a main branch can cross the trunk or another branch in order to produce a dramatic effect or to project a sense of the tree's freedom. Most Literati trees have triangular crowns and foliage clusters that harmonize with each other.

driftwood literati

Juniperus horizontalis Glauca Group is a groundcover plant with horizontal spreading branches. Instead of growing this species in the normal way, the tree shown left was deliberately planted upright after its first year of horizontal growth. This unnatural method of cultivation results in pendulous branching. The illustration shows a mature specimen with a gentle curving trunk.

To the bonsai grower, the tree seemed to have hidden potential, so it was carefully studied all round and at various angles. Three big branches growing at its apex were converted into tien jin that would dominate the design. When the apical branches were jinned, the resulting tien jin was slanting (see page 94, top). Tien in both Chinese and Japanese means "heaven," so a tien jin should always be vertical.

With the tien jin as the focal point, the movement of the trunk would have greater dramatic impact once the jin was connected

ABOVE The stem of a Literati bends sharply before splitting into two limbs at its apex.

BELOW When a ground-hugging juniper is grown upright, its apical branches droop dramatically.

to a shari (see page 124) in the trunk. A main branch that could be shaped into a crown to harmonize with the trunk line was selected just below the tien jin, and some of the smaller branches in the crown were eliminated and the rest wired.

When deciding on the front of a Literati, the initial movement of the trunk has to be taken into consideration (see below left). From there the sweeping movement of the shari on the trunk would give an impression of momentum propelling the tree upwards. The tree then diverges into a crown, while the shari curves gracefully towards the apex. Near the top it divides into separate piercing jins, while branches in the crown were shaped into an Informal Upright style. A thick rubber band was tied around the crown to bring it closer to its remarkable driftwood trunk.

The shari on this tien jin bonsai was carved gradually out of the live bark. To start with, about five years ago, a strip of bark, about a fifth of an inch (4mm) wide, was peeled off the trunk. Further strips, about a tenth of an inch (2mm) wide, were removed from the length of the trunk a few times a year. The shari ended about a fifth of an inch (4mm) above the soil surface. If it had been extended into the soil, it would have been difficult to prevent the exposed area from rotting. This daring Driftwood Literati was designed to look austere. Its trunk movement starts off subtly at first, becoming powerful and dramatic as it approaches its apex.

neglected garden plant

The *Rhododendrum impeditum* branches profusely and is normally sold at garden centers when it is about 8 inches (20cm) high. It blooms twice a year, in spring and early fall. If

ABOVE LEFT **A jinned apex with driftwood sweeping down like a calligraphic brushstroke along the length of the juniper's trunk would dominates this bunjin.**

BELOW LEFT **Attractive driftwood should be complemented with a minimum amount of foliage in the crown.**

RIGHT **The implicit trunk movement of this Literati clearly demonstrates the determination to overcome neglect and flower profusely.**

left unpruned, old plants can reach a height of more than 20 inches (50cm).

The example on page 95 is a Literati that is 22 inches (55cm) tall and was found in a garden that had been left to grow wild. Its lower branches had died off because of shading and competition from neighboring plants and after 10 years of neglect, its crown consisted of only two main branches. The left branch was the higher one, so it had to be the main branch. The other branch was deliberately lowered by bending it with wire towards the back and then towards the front. Foliage on the secondary branch was slightly reduced to integrate it into an asymmetric crown. The delicate movement in this Literati was matched to a Chinese pot with curved feet. It is unusual to see a Literati covered with lilac-colored flowers, but this colorful display lasts only a few weeks. For the rest of the year its elegant trunk takes center stage—a real symbol of survival.

restyling a reject

One of the most stimulating aspects of cultivating bonsai is the possibility of changing the look of one that has already been trained. About 12 years ago the design of this Literati style Chinese juniper (above left) had not been carefully conceived. Its crown was too heavy in comparison to the long, thin trunk . Something was needed to infuse an element of dynamism in it. The trunk could be drastically shortened, down to its lowest branch, but that particular branch would not constitute an interesting crown, so two other branches above it, the left and front branches, were brought together to form an integrated crown that harmonized with the delicate movement of the trunk. As you can see from the lower picture—when the trunk was inclined to a 45-degree angle, the branch on the left had to visually balance the slant and the front branch was required to counterbalance the foliage mass on the left.

After refining the tree for two years, it was planted in a large, shallow pot to give stability to the slanting trunk. Although the curves in the trunk are very gentle, its prominent bark seems to instill a sense of robustness in the tree. The result of this restyling is a more elegant Literati (opposite).

OPPOSITE TOP When the crown of a bonsai seems too heavy in comparison to its long, thin trunk, restyling can restore the balance.

OPPOSITE BELOW The elimination of unnecessary branches reduced the tree to a simple balanced framework. Only two branches were left to form a neat crown in proportion to the leaning trunk.

BELOW A few years later, "clouds" of foliage in an asymmetric crown keep the slanting trunk well balanced.

hobbit style trees

In contrast to the normal bonsai convention of cultivating soil-hugging surface roots, Hobbit style tree roots are deliberately exposed to create hollows, as in the film *The Lord of the Rings* where the hobbits took refuge in the roots of the trees. These hollows may be seen in nature. Trees growing in areas where soil is frequently eroded, for example by riverbanks or gullies, develop tenacious roots that thicken as they are constantly flushed by the running water. The cavern-like holes that form beneath these tree trunks have a mysterious look (left). Unusually, this intriguing Zen aspect focuses on one of the least dominant features of a bonsai.

Similarly, in the tropics, a fig seedling growing on another tree can, after several decades, completely envelop its host with its serpentine roots. Under the dominant canopy of the vigorous fig, the host tree will struggle to survive and more often than not, it will eventually give up. Within the web of roots of the aptly named Strangling fig, the trunk of the dead tree will finally decay, leaving a hollow for owls and bushbabies to nestle in.

creating a hollow with exposed roots

To create a Hobbit style bonsai, you need a tree with a massive trunk and a low crown; large, sturdy roots to create the hollow under the trunk; small leaves, and heavy lower branches. The tree also needs to be a vigorous grower that can withstand drastic pruning and achieve good branching in a relatively short time, say two to three years.

A young elm, a Trident maple (*Acer buergerianum*) or a fig tree with many long, flexible roots makes a good choice. All the roots must be untangled and studied to see how to create the hollow under the trunk. Next, the stump of a dead tree that is likely to rot away in three to five years is needed. Prune off all its roots and shape the stump to a size that will allow the roots of the future Hobbit style tree to grow over it. The front of the bonsai should be selected at this stage because the exact position of the entrance to the cave must be determined. Now arrange the roots neatly over the stump and bind them securely to it with lots of strips of cloth. Ugly, badly positioned roots may be removed provided there are sufficient feeder roots left to sustain the tree. If there are any mature, woody roots that are too rigid, wire them carefully with tissue-wrapped aluminum wires and bend them to shape over the stump.

In spring, transplant the tree into a large pot or into the ground. The exposed roots should rise above the soil surface. Allow the tree to grow unchecked for at least five years, pruning only the most vigorous shoots to ensure they do not mar the basic shape. Before the exposed roots start fusing with each other, insert wooden wedges between them to separate those roots at the entrance to the cave. When most of the remaining roots have fused together, transplant the tree into a bonsai pot. Re-adjust the roots as necessary where possible. Look at the beautiful example (opposite below) of a fig-tree bonsai trained in this manner.

The branches of the bonsai can be shaped by pruning and wiring to harmonize with its exposed roots. Crooked hanging branches would help create an eerie feeling. This can be achieved by pruning, using the clip and grow technique. On the other hand, if the roots are sinuous, the branch configuration should be curving rather than crooked.

a secret cavern for hobbits

A quicker alternative to the above method is to locate a bonsai that already has a number of very large exposed roots. Chinese bonsai growers are very fond of cultivating trees like this and they are often exported to Western Europe where they are sold as indoor bonsai. Choose one with an unblemished trunk and with a beautiful movement of the trunk, and see if the branches arise from ideal bends in the tree. Another option is to explore the possibility of using a large branch at the lower end of the trunk to create a low crown. This can be accomplished by reduction pruning—that is the reduction of the height of a bonsai by eliminating the top portion of the stem.

The Chinese elm (*Zelkova schneideria*) shown right was specially chosen for its powerful lower trunk and enormous grasping roots. It already had a "secret cavern" hidden under the trunk. When the lowest branch on the left was looked at carefully, a suprising discovery was made. It would be possible

OPPOSITE, TOP **A captivating opening into the inner recesses of a tree.**

OPPOSITE, BELOW **When the roots of a Strangling fig (*Ficus watkinsiana*) finally enclose its host, the tree is squeezed to death, leaving a cryptic hollow.**

BELOW **Bonsai growers in China are fond of cultivating trees with interesting root systems. This elm has enormous robust roots sheltering a cavern.**

to remove the stem above the junction where this branch articulated from the trunk and use the branch to substitute for the rest of the tree growing above. In other words, the branch had sufficient limbs to form a new crown. In addition, a reasonably good taper would be obtained after amputation of the stem, while the movement of the lowest branch could be made to harmonize with the curving trunk line.

The roots of the elm were carefully exposed (left), and the stem was amputated at a slant with a saw. Patient sawing ensured a clean cut, then a shallow groove was carved along the edge of the cut to facilitate rapid healing. The wound was then covered with cut paste (see page 156). A large horizontal root pointing to the right was shortened, and other awkwardly growing roots were neatly untangled. An assessment of the roots made it possible to decide on the choice of pot. The container needed to allow the exposed roots to be displayed but also had to match the size and style of the tree. As the root system was surprisingly small, the elm was easily transplanted into its new home with minimum root pruning. It was positioned on a mound of well-draining soil and a number of small branches were eliminated, while others were pruned and shaped with wire. Next, the posture of the tree was adjusted to show the entrance into the cavern (below left).

Finally, Chinese lily turf (*Ophiopogon*) was planted between the roots on the left-hand side to enhance the height of the tree and sedum was planted at the back of the cavern to add some depth to the scene. After four weeks, the vigorous elm branched profusely (opposite). Meticulous pruning of the secondary and tertiary branches was done to develop crooked branching in

ABOVE LEFT A massive trunk with a low crown and hanging branches draws attention to its colossal grasping roots, so the trunk was drastically shortened down to its lowest branch.

BELOW LEFT After wire-shaping the arching branch into a crown, the elm was precisely positioned in the pot to display its most intriguing feature—a secret cavern.

OPPOSITE A profusion of adventitious budding and rampant growth enabled the rapid formation of an impressive canopy for the Hobbit tree.

bonsai
techniques

basic maintenance

Literally translated bonsai means "planted in a pot." The tree can be maintained in a healthy condition only if its horticultural requirements are properly understood. It is shaped and kept artificially small with training techniques.

horticultural requirements

position

In spring and fall, most species of tree should be exposed to plenty of sun and air, but the majority of broad-leaved outdoor bonsai should be shaded with netting against strong summer sun, while conifers with needles appreciate full exposure to the sun. Tender maples prefer a shady location protected from drying wind. Below, sun-loving Chinese juniper and pine bonsai are placed on the top of a high shelving unit, while a

BELOW In the garden of a bonsai grower, a well-ventilated, protected area should be set aside where bonsai can be easily tended. Conifers may be exposed to a lot of sunshine but Japanese maples prefer dappled shade.

Japanese maple is displayed in a shadier position. A bonsai should be rotated once every few days so that every part of the tree is exposed to sunlight. See Overwintering (page 109) for information on where to keep bonsai in winter.

soil

The essential properties of bonsai soil concern water retention, porosity, nutrient retention, and acidity. Most plants will grow in a soil with a pH between 5.5 and 6.5. Growers should know the specific requirement of each bonsai with regards to the acidity, porosity, and moisture-retaining qualities of its soil mixture. Pine trees and junipers excavated from arid regions (see right) cannot tolerate wet feet, so should be planted in a very porous mixture, while a swamp cypress bonsai (*Taxodium distichum*) does not mind being saturated with water in summer, so a mixture that retains moisture is more desirable. Local weather can also influence the composition of a soil mixture.

According to an American Bonsai Society survey, the most popular soil mixture consists of equal volumes of coarse sand, topsoil or humus, and baked clay. One experienced British bonsai grower uses equal parts of pumice, calcined/baked clay and Cornish grit—all sieved. In Japan, most growers prefer only Akadama (see page 156) or three parts Akadama to one part grit. Akadama consists of baked clay granules with a neutral pH of 6.9 but a low C.E.C. (see page 156), so regular feeding is necessary. Due to its good draining and moisture-retaining qualities, it is exported to many countries and is popular with bonsai growers.

ABOVE Bonsai trees grow in various types of soil in different parts of the world. An excavated Californian juniper will recover and generate new roots in moist gravel. Wet soil would kill the tree.

watering

A bonsai should be watered slowly until excess water flows out of the drainage holes. When a bonsai is flowering or fruiting it needs more frequent watering, but over-watering can lead to root rot and death. On warm, windy days the humidity of the soil can decline rapidly so regular checking is necessary. You can see if the soil is dry as it will be lighter in color and weight. If in doubt, poke your finger in about a third of an inch. If the soil is dry your finger will be quite clean or coated with a little soil

ABOVE In the growing season, underwatering for just one day could result in drooping leaves. On the other hand, if a conifer is not watered for several days it may not show any sign of damage initially, but several weeks later, its needles will turn brown.

dust. If the soil is dry, water immediately as dry roots lead to brown needles or leaves (left), or to permanent loss of branches. Once the leaves droop, the bonsai will be stressed. Watering should be carried out preferably early in the morning or late in the afternoon.

A Mame bonsai has special requirements. Its leaves or needles have to be kept as small as possible so these small bonsai are watered only when the soil is about 90 per cent dry.

Avoid the habit of pouring small amounts of water now and then on the soil as this encourages feeder roots to proliferate near the surface. If the surface is not covered with a layer of moss, these hairy roots will be vulnerable to drying out. In addition, the feeder roots will not allow water to penetrate deeper in the soil to reach the mass of roots lower down the pot. If these roots dry out and die, the branches of the tree will die too.

Whenever possible, use rainwater and if that is not available, leave tap water to stand in the watering can for a day to enable the chlorine gas to escape. The disadvantage of using too much tap water is its alkalinity. This denies nutrients to acid-loving plants and also leads to an accumulation of chalk along the rim of the pot and sometimes on the sides of the container. To decrease the alkalinity of tap water, it can be passed very slowly through a sieve containing peat moss.

Trees in nature that are exposed to many years of acid rain get weak and grow susceptible to disease so they gradually degenerate and die. A tree growing in a bonsai pot escapes this damage because its soil has to be renewed periodically.

feeding

The three main components of fertilizer are nitrogen (N), phosphorous (P), and potassium (K). Different amounts of each must be supplied to a tree depending on the stage of its training. A fertilizer with a high nitrogen content will encourage luxuriant growth, which is important if you are trying to increase the girth of the trunk. More phosphorous and potassium will encourage flowering and the development of fruits. They also harden tender shoots and roots in fall in preparation for a cold winter.

Cottonseed meal contains nitrogen, phosphorus and potassium in the ratio 5:3:1. Bonemeal is made from ground-up animal bones and its main ingredient is phosphoric acid. Bloodmeal is pulverized animal blood. It contains 13 per cent nitrogen and promotes the rapid growth of foliage. Both can easily be mixed in the soil during transplanting. Trace elements such as iron, zinc, magnesium, copper, and so on, occur naturally in organic fertilizers but must be specifically included in commercial organic or chemical fertilizers.

This neglected bougainvillea (right) has produced leaves that are discolored, weak, and curly. Its soil should be changed and its roots examined. If the roots are still healthy, the problem could be poor feeding. A light, general fertilizer should be applied to the bonsai about a month after transplantation to strengthen the tree.

One type of organic fertilizer in pellet form, known as Bio Gold, is specially manufactured for bonsai and is exported from Japan. Most brands are now impregnated with an insecticide to kill insect larvae. Any product that contains three parts cottonseed meal, one part bonemeal and five parts bloodmeal will be good for rapid growth and improvement in the flowering and fruiting capacity of a bonsai.

The dosage depends on the season, the species of the tree, its size and age. For instance, a chemical fertilizer with a ratio of 5N:10P:10K will inhibit strong luxuriant growth of a fully trained bonsai, which could prevent fine ramification. Another commercial fertilizer specially manufactured for conifers is in the ratio 15N:5P:10K plus 4 of magnesium oxide. This trace element prevents premature browning of the foliage and should be applied in early spring and early summer, followed by a tomato feed (0N:11P:11K) in fall. Soluble fertilizer is quick acting while organic fertilizer takes about 10 days to be absorbed. Do not apply fertilizer in summer if the temperature rises above 27 degrees Celcius.

pests and diseases

Multi-purpose sprays to rid plants of most pests can be purchased at garden centers. There are also sprays for fungal

ABOVE Do not fertilize a tree if it is diseased. Only treat for iron deficiency (apparent if the leaves are pale and highlighted by green nerves). In all other cases, consult an expert to determine the lack of trace elements or the type of disease.

diseases but other, more serious, diseases should be diagnozed by an expert before a remedy is sought. Fungi often attack plants over-wintering in damp, poorly ventilated locations. Some of the most troublesome pests, such as certain aphids and mites, hatch in spring and can reach plague proportions if left unchecked. In order to prevent this, all bonsai should be sprayed with lime sulfur, first at the end of fall, after the leaves have dropped, and then in early spring. Lime sulfur is an insecticide and a fungicide. It should be diluted with 20–30 parts of water.

During the growing season, it is necessary to be vigilant for pests and diseases and to check all bonsai thoroughly at least once a week. You may find it more convenient to treat certain plants with a systemic insecticide. This is absorbed into every part of the tree so that any sucking insects will be poisoned when they attack. Tablets containing a systemic insecticide can be inserted into the soil (follow the manufacturer's instructions).

transplanting

Sometimes a bonsai shows signs of weakening, for example it starts to wither. This could be due to blocked drainage holes trapping water in the pot and rotting the roots or it could be caused by a compacted root system and an insufficiently moisture-retentive soil. The roots of a bonsai can spread to fill its container completely in a few years (below left), so it is important to transplant the tree before they start to grow out of the drainage holes or when they begin to emerge above the surface of the soil.

Before repotting, prune off about a third in volume of the root system and shorten the long, thick roots to promote the growth of feeder roots. All large cuts should be sealed with a waterproof wound sealant. Carefully remove as much of the old soil as possible from the container and replace with a well-draining mixture.

The frequency of transplanting depends on the training plan of the bonsai but in general young trees should be repotted more often than older trees. Fast-growing species that produce abundant roots, such as boxwood or elms, may be transplanted

BELOW To check if a bonsai needs repotting, ease the tree from its pot by sliding a knife along the edge. If the mass of roots contains almost no soil it must be repotted as soon as possible.

in alternate years, whereas less vigorous old pines may be transplanted every three to five years. The long-neglected white pine (right) had not been transplanted for at least 10 years.

The best time to transplant a tree is when the leafbuds (not the flowerbuds) are swelling and about to open. Flowering bonsai like azaleas, wisterias, and forsythias should be transplanted after flowering. Remove all decaying blooms at the same time. Fruit-bearing bonsai such as quinces, apples, and apricots should be transplanted in fall, while conifers should be transplanted, for preference, in spring.

overwintering

In temperate climates, as long as the temperature does not go more than a few degrees below freezing, winter-hardy bonsai may be left outdoors without protection. Check the moisture content of the soil of evergreen trees. If the weather was dry for several days prior to the freeze and the soil is well drained, the root system of the bonsai will not be harmed.

Semi-tropical bonsai are less winter hardy, but they benefit from short periods of light frost (not exceeding three degrees) before being transferred to their winter quarters. This triggers their biological clocks to prepare them for dormancy.

If, on the other hand, the soil is not well-drained and is very wet due to heavy rain prior to the freeze, then the root system could be damaged by prolonged frost. Put the bonsai in an unheated room, for example a cellar, attic, or garage and try to drain the excess water by tilting the pot on one side for anything from several hours to a day, depending on the size of the tree. Next, remove the pot and wrap the rootball in absorbent material such as newspaper, and then in an old woollen garment. Root rot is the most serious threat to the life of a bonsai.

Deciduous species of bonsai can be overwintered in a room with a temperature of 0–4 degrees Celcius without light, but natural light should be provided for evergreen trees. Do not panic if the outdoor temperature falls more than a few degrees below freezing. Simply provide extra protection for the rootball and/or pot if a prolonged colder freeze is expected. A maximum-

ABOVE In exceptional cases, pines and junipers, even though not repotted for a long time, seem to remain healthy. Unfortunately, after a decade, it would be extremely difficult and tedious to root-prune these bonsai.

minimum thermometer is essential to monitor temperature changes. Check the humidity of the soil weekly. It should be just moist, not constantly wet. Depending on the environment, some bonsai will require watering only once a month. Provide ventilation to prevent fungal attacks.

In early spring, the soft shoots of less hardy varieties of Japanese maples, *Kadsura japonica,* and *Leptospermum* can be damaged by frost or cold drying winds. At this time tropical bonsai that are kept indoors should be exposed to plenty of daylight and humidity, for example on a kitchen or bathroom windowsill (left). After dark, try and give them extra artificial (fluorescent) lighting to increase their exposure to 12 hours a day. At the end of spring, when nighttime temperatures do not drop below 10 degrees Celcius, these indoor bonsai should be gradually exposed to outdoor conditions. Hardy bonsai, with or without their pot, may be buried in the ground throughout the winter. The rootball should be totally covered with soil, then topped with a layer of dead leaves or pine needles to a depth of at least a third of an inch (7mm).

shaping

The two most popular and effective ways of shaping a bonsai are pruning and wiring. The aims of pruning are:

Dwarfing – A bonsai tree is kept small by constant pruning of its branches.

Ramification – To maintain a bonsai at a reduced scale, its branches must be ramified so that it looks like an mature, lofty tree.

Balancing vigor – The vigorous growth of the outer branches must be controlled by pruning to allow more energy to be channeled to the latter.

Structural shaping – The basic structure of a bonsai is obtained after eliminating superfluous branches by "heavy" pruning.

After carefully determining the "front" of a nursery plant grown in a container/training pot, superfluous branches are pruned off and wired in order to achieve the required bonsai structure. Thereafter, the retained branches are encouraged to produce secondary and tertiary branches by selective pruning. Subsequently, peripheral branches must be ramified by a"hard" pruning to produce fine twigs. Finally, the fully trained bonsai is kept small by constant "soft" pruning of shoots that extend outside the desired crown profile.

pruning

One of the methods of creating the basic shape of a bonsai is the removal of unnecessary branches. This is done by heavy pruning, grooming, soft pruning, and hard pruning.

HEAVY PRUNING

Areas of strong growth have to be restrained by the removal of thick branches, and areas of congested branching must be thinned out in order to allow more light to reach interior branches in the canopy. Thick branches may be cut with a concave cutter, pruning shears or a small saw (below, far right). Any pruned branch that is thicker than the diameter of a pencil should be covered with cut paste to protect the exposed cambium tissue.

OPPOSITE **An ideal environment to overwinter an indoor bonsai is on the bright windowsill of a bathroom where it is both warm and humid.**

BELOW **Basic bonsai tools from left to right: wire cutter, scissors for clipping, concave cutter for heavy pruning, jin pliers, hand saw for heavy pruning.**

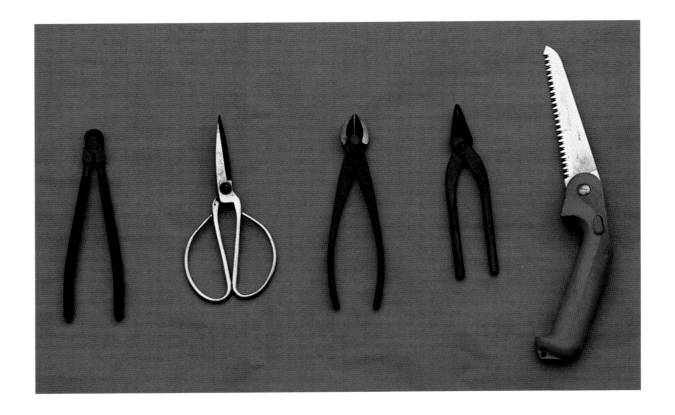

After being neglected for many years, the white pine (left) produced numerous branches. In order to shape the tree into a bonsai, a concave cutter was used to cut off unwanted branches and the result can be seen below.

The heavy pruning of pines, maples, birches, and other nut-bearing trees should be carried out in winter as these species bleed profusely from cut wounds in the growing season. Streaks of resin ooze out that look extremely unsightly on a pine tree. A large-diameter cut should not be made flush against the trunk. In the first winter, the lower half of the branch should be cut off and a callus allowed to form. The following winter, the rest of the branch can be pruned off entirely using a concave cutter. This method will prevent sap withdrawal from under the branch, which would kill the roots. All species of trees pruned in winter should be protected from frost.

GROOMING

On a fully trained bonsai, distinctive foliage clusters have to be kept in shape by grooming. All growth emerging out of and spoiling the line of a properly shaped foliage cluster must be removed. Inspect and prune off any wild-growing shoots from all sides as well as from above the bonsai. The picture opposite, above left, shows how the emerging shoots of a Japanese maple are immediately plucked off to two leaves with a pincer.

SOFT PRUNING (OR FINGER-PINCHING)

Hornbeam (*Carpinus*) bonsai tend to produce large leaves. This is not desirable on a well-ramified tree, so as soon as soft shoots appear, allow only two leaves to remain on each new shoot and finger-pinch the rest (opposite, above right). In this way growth will be curtailed at the periphery and the leaves will be smaller.

ABOVE LEFT **The neglected white pine before heavy pruning of the unwanted branches.**

BELOW LEFT **After pruning, the selected branches on both sides of the leaning trunk were arranged by wire-shaping to keep the tree esthetically in balance.**

In the growing season, the fast-growing varieties of elms have to be pinched once a week to encourage ramification. Most other broad-leaved species are pinched about once a month. This aspect is especially important for small bonsai. A shohin bonsai without fine branching would fail to impart the illusion of a large, old tree.

Except for pines, evergreens with needles should be finger-pinched to remove half of every emerging needle cluster. The candles of pines should be pinched to about a third of their length in spring when they start to lengthen. If these candles are allowed to develop into shoots, back budding can be stimulated by shortening the terminal branches down to a dormant bud in late summer. Excessive growth of needles must be plucked off in late fall or early spring before bud activity starts (see right).

HARD PRUNING

Long, woody shoots with large internodes must be shortened by cutting them down to two leaves with a pair of scissors. Note that the last dormant bud on each pruned branch will determine the direction of its new terminal. If this is not borne in mind, new shoots will end up crossing each other.

ABOVE LEFT To control growth within a well-ramified crown, all soft shoots must be shortened to one pair of leaves.

ABOVE RIGHT Regular pinching of soft shoots to two leaves ramifies twigs to produce smaller leaves.

BELOW By reducing excessive growth of pine needles on stronger branches, the tree channels more energy into weaker branches.

No more than two dormant buds should be allowed to grow at each internode or "witch's brooms" (old, thickened multiple twigs) will develop and mar the silhouette of a well-groomed canopy. The space between the internodes of a branch should get less as the branch extends towards the periphery of the crown. Hard pruning should be done in summer.

DEFOLIATION

This is another technique that encourages ramification on a deciduous tree. It involves cutting off all the leaves, except those on weak branches, in mid-summer (between the end of June and the second week of July). Leaves with short petioles should not be pulled off because their dormant buds may be wrenched out in the process. The leaves of elms and maples (below) should be cut off with a pair of scissors. Once the tree has been stripped of its leaves, more sunlight will be able to penetrate the inner parts of the crown and stimulate the growth of dormant buds. During this period, make sure that the soil is kept moist but not wet. When new shoots appear, they should be reduced to one or two leaves by soft pruning. These new leaves will be smaller because the tree has been forced to produce double the quantity of foliage from its year's energy reserve. For this reason, defoliation should only be carried out every other year and only if the tree is in excellent health. A fruiting bonsai must never be defoliated because it will flower again and the tree will weaken.

wiring

There are a number of basic rules to follow concerning the shaping of a bonsai with wires. You should always work in front of the bonsai at eye-level, because that is how all bonsai should be viewed, and you should commence wiring from the bottom of the tree to the top and from its interior to the periphery. Wherever possible, wires should not cross each other and they should all coil in one direction. Following these guidelines will ensure that the wires can easily be removed from the bonsai.

The most effective angle at which a wire should be coiled round a branch is 45 degrees. Make sure the wire just touches the surface of the branch. If it is wired too tightly the wire will mark

BELOW To encourage well-structured branching, secondary or tertiary shoots are allowed to lengthen and lignify before they are shortened with scissors.

the bark as the branch thickens. Conversely, a loosely wired branch cannot be properly bent as the wire does not have enough grip, and there will be a greater risk of the branch breaking. The relative thickness of wire and branch are also important. The photograph shows aluminum wires of various thicknesses conveniently coiled round spools in a crate. When using aluminum wires, the wire should be half the thickness of the branch, but as copper wire is more rigid, it should be about a third that of the branch. A copper wire should be annealed to make it more flexible. When wiring a long branch, the thickness of the wire should be reduced as the branch tapers.

Practice bending twigs and branches (with or without wiring) obtained from hedges and trees before you bend bonsai stems. Familiarize yourself with the amount of pressure required to bend, but not break, branches of different thicknesses. Listen intently in case a branch begins to crack. If a coiled branch is cracked but not completely broken, apply egg white or cut paste to the wound and leave it to heal (see page 121).

In general, the best time to wire most species of trees is in fall, after leaves have dropped, and in winter. In spring and summer the bark of conifers tends to separate from the live tissue when a branch is bent or twisted, so wire-shaping of conifers during these seasons could result in dead branches. The wiring on a conifer bonsai may be left on the tree for up to about a year but the wires on a broad-leaved bonsai should be removed after a few months, before scarring can occur. If a Japanese maple bonsai is wired in the active growing season, its bark could be marked within several weeks, so be vigilant.

1 COILING WIRE ON A BRANCH

To wire a branch, hold the junction firmly with one hand, then coil wire round the branch with the index finger and thumb of the other hand. When a coiled branch is to be bent, grip the branch with both hands and apply pressure gradually and in a controlled manner. Normally, branches are bent downwards so observe the top surface of the bark as it stretches. When hairline splits appear, cease bending.

2 WIRING TWO BRANCHES

Coiling two branches of a similar thickness with one wire. These two branches should be growing out at different heights along the trunk so the wire can initially be anchored somewhere behind the trunk or coiled around it.

clouds

In Japanese art, pine trees are usually drawn with branches of foliage that look like "clouds." A well-balanced assembly of these clouds constitute an idealized portrayal in the canopy of a pine bonsai.

Examples of foliage "clouds" are portrayed on a classical pine-tree painting.

1 The weaker branches of this pine were allowed to grow more foliage for a year. The terminals of these branches point upwards to gain strength.

2 After wiring the principal branches with 3/20-inch (3mm) and 1/5-inch (4mm) wires, they were lowered by bending.

3 The longest branch on the left, viewed from above. It was pre-trained by pruning and wiring about two years ago.

4 The wired branch shaped into foliage "clouds."

more advanced skills

BELOW **If the bonsai clamp is used properly, a precise bend can be created gradually on a branch or trunk.**

The basic training of a bonsai involves various pruning techniques coupled with standard methods of wiring. However, some trees require the bending of very thick branches or the carving of parts of the trunk into driftwood. These complicated techniques should be used only when simple solutions cannot be found.

N.B Power tools should be handled with great care. An accidental slip during the carving of a shari can cause a nasty wound. In most bonsai clubs there are always enthusiasts eager to share their new techniques and improvisations, but only tried and tested devices and training techniques should be presented there.

using a bonsai clamp

This special device comes in various sizes from 2–12 inches (5–30cm), but the larger ones are used more often. A large clamp can straighten the curved trunk of a tree if it is not too rigid. Alternatively, it could be used to create a precise bend on a straight trunk.

The upper trunk of this tamarisk (left) looks as though it is stuck on top of an old stump. To improve the tree's design, a clamp could be fixed to the supple stem to create a bend just below the place where the trunk starts to branch out. The lowest branch on the left would then articulate elegantly above the curve in the stem. The curve must be created gradually by turning the spindle on the screw about a quarter turn once a month during the growing season. (In the dormant period the stem would be too rigid). If pressure is applied too hastily, the stem could fracture. The clamp should be in position for one to two years to ensure a permanent curvature. Use rubber or plastic foam padding to protect the thin bark of the tamarisk.

using chopsticks

On a Broom style tree, some branches may be too close to others when viewed from the front. Instead of wiring whole branches to separate them further, the distance between two branches can be fixed by simply wedging a chopstick in between. The chopstick is first measured against one branch (opposite) and then cut off with a rounded concave cutter at the other end against the other branch. A concave cut on the stick allows the cut edge to push against the round surface of the branch without slipping. The opposite end of the chopstick should also be trimmed a little with the rounded concave cutter so that it will fit comfortably against the other branch.

BELOW A well-spaced network of branches can easily be created by wedging neighboring branches with different lengths of chopstick.

ABOVE **Branches may be lowered gradually with the aid of guy wires.**

using guy wires

If a very thick branch cannot be lowered by wiring alone, a guy wire can effectively pull the limb down to the required level. A strong wire passed through an opening in a coiled branch should be anchored preferably to a steel bar fastened to the surface of the pot (above left). Guy wires can also be attached to the top and bottom of a double-screw to lower the branch gradually over a period of several months (above right).

restoring a fractured branch

Every time a fairly thick branch is bent, there is a risk of it breaking. It may be that it was not wired correctly, that insufficient wire was wound round the branch, that the wrong gauge of wire was used, that an incorrect bending technique was used, or that the branch was bent too hastily or without sufficient care.

When bending a heavy branch, the wired branch must be supported with one hand while pressure is slowly applied, first with the palm of the other hand, then with both palms. The convex (or tensile) surface of the branch should be watched for hairline cracks and sounds of cracking should be listened for intently. As soon as hairline cracks appear on the bark, you should stop bending. If a crack is heard, check whether the branch is partially fractured or completely broken. If it is only partially fractured, i.e. less than one third of the diameter of the limb has been separated, leave it in that position and apply cut paste or egg white to the damaged area. If it is more damaged than that but has not broken completely, you should bend it back slowly towards its original position as much as possible. Apply cut paste or egg white to the fractured area, then wrap the branch tightly with raffia. The broken ends will callus over but, unlike broken bone, broken wood does not fuse together. Once it has been damaged in this way, a branch must not be bent again even after it has healed. Alas, a completely broken branch cannot be restored and an alternative solution must be sought.

using reinforced wires in raffia to bend a heavy branch

Curves on large branches are normally obtained by coiling several thick wires parallel to each other round the branch and then bending the branch. However, when a curve is desired on an exceptionally large and heavy branch, it is better to use reinforced wires in raffia. This technique is often applied to species with flexible branches such as pines or junipers. It is rarely used on maples and azaleas, which are very brittle.

Natural, rather than plastic, raffia soaked in water shrinks after drying. When strands of wet raffia are wound on a branch, the shrinkage prevents the bark and living tissues from detaching from the heartwood (top right).

Four wires, about a fifth the diameter of the branch are laid horizontally along the surface of the branch. These wires give additional support to the branch as it is being bent and help prevent it from breaking. In the centre, another layer of wet raffia is being wound around the horizontal wires and the branch to hold them in position. Finally, one or more heavy wires are wound around the branch before it is bent (below right). Spring and fall are the best seasons to perform this bending technique. After bending, protect the bonsai from strong sun and wind for two weeks. If the soil is on the dry side, water generously, making sure you wet the foliage too.

TOP To bend a heavy branch, first wrap the branch with raffia to protect the cambium and bark.

CENTER Attach two wires along both sides of the branch, as well as a third wire above, and a fourth wire below the branch.

BELOW Wrap several strands of raffia tightly around the branch. Coil thick wires around the branch, then commence bending.

to bend a very thick branch

In the pine tree on page 117, the back branch was almost as long and thick as the principal branch. It was growing from a less than ideal position, not at the back of the trunk, but more towards the left side of the stem. Initially, this fault was camouflaged by a front branch. However, the branch could be bent further towards the back and downwards with the aid of the reinforced wires in raffia technique, plus a reduction of heartwood on one side of the branch.

1 A portion of wood in the back branch had to be carved out to make it less rigid. Viewed from behind, the back branch needed bending towards the left, so a horizontal cavity had to be carved out on the compression (left) side of the limb, near the base of that branch.

2 A high-speed router was used to remove wood to a depth of about half the diameter of the branch and to a length equal to at least three times the thickness of the branch. The exposed cambium at the edges of the cavity was protected with cut paste.

3 Raffia soaked in water beforehand was laid lengthwise in the cavity, wrapped around the trunk and then over the branch cavity.

4 Four fairly thick wires were laid horizontally next to the raffia-covered crevice as shown in this photograph. Several strands of raffia were again wound tightly around the branch, back towards the trunk and then around the trunk.

5 Afterwards, the cavity was covered with a third layer of raffia and the branch was neatly wired with 1/5-inch (4mm) wires. Finally, the branch was bent slowly and held in position with the aid of a turnbuckle. These suspended wires should be of copper or steel, not of aluminum, which would easily break under tension. It will take about two years for the branch to hold its new position. If everything were dismantled within a year, the branch would spring back to its original position.

using carving tools

Since the 1980s, Driftwood style bonsai have captured the imagination of many bonsai artists, but producing them requires considerable skill and knowledge, as well as the use of special carving tools. The hard wood of juniper, cedar, spruce, yew, or fir are suitable candidates as they can be preserved artificially for a long time. Most varieties of broad-leaved trees

RIGHT A partially debarked trunk, exposes the rustic beauty and fighting spirit of a tree.

OPPOSITE ABOVE Heavy, redundant branches that are excluded from the design of a bonsai could be carved to simulate driftwood weathered by nature.

OPPOSITE BELOW After debarking, strips of wood carefully torn off a thick branch could reveal an interesting, fissured shari.

rot easily, except for the heartwood of oak and boxwood. Pine trees will bleed unless their bark is stripped in the dormant season and dead branches on Japanese maples are often susceptible to fungal diseases so shari is not recommended.

Because coniferous wood is fibrous, strips of wood can be wrenched off a trunk with pliers to reveal its grain. Amazing areas of driftwood can be carved out of debarked branches with power tools (right), though care must be taken because in unskilled hands, the results can look artificial. Drills, rasps, and grinders are required for the detailing of jins and sharis. In many instances, these natural effects can also be imitated with the help of a sharp knife, a concave pruner, a burin, and a pair of jin pliers. When a branch is wrenched off the trunk with jin pliers, the texture of the wood left on the lacerated stem looks more natural than when it is carved. Patient stripping of wood, fiber by fiber, from a debarked area will produce contrasting details on the sharis (below right).

After they have been created, jins and sharis must be preserved with lime sulfur solution, originally manufactured for killing hibernating pests and for the prevention of fungal infections (see page 108). If the jins or sharis look too white, add a drop of black watercolor paint to the solution to dull the brightness. When it is being applied, be sure to protect the surface of the soil to prevent this aggressive chemical from damaging the bonsai roots. You should also protect all exposed cambium with cut paste (see page 122).

Plant material that has already been damaged in some way lends itself to this type of treatment. Some of the trunks of nursery plants that have previously been shaped into bonsai are often scarred by pruning cuts. The bark covering these areas can be stripped off to reveal the beautiful scars beneath. Unintended wire markings and other traumas that have disfigured thick branches leave interesting details that can be exposed to advantage. Many neglected nursery plants also suffer from damage. Lacerations, for example, can be made into exquisite effects. Such plants as well as material with numerous, chaotic branches are ideal for the creation of driftwood.

second chance for a Chinese juniper

About 10 years ago, an unusual nursery plant was acquired because it had a slight hollow in its trunk. After pruning it was shaped into an Informal Upright bonsai. During the bending process one of its main branches was accidentally damaged so further shaping was discontinued. The tree was planted in shady ground and neglected for many years. Without sufficient exposure to the sun and proper feeding, growth was slow but the juniper was not unhealthy. It was considered for conversion into a shari-kan on a number of occasions. The most attractive feature of this tree was its slight hollow. If this could be combined with driftwood, the juniper trunk would dominate the bonsai. The tree would also need to feature a subordinate crown to complement the driftwood. One option seemed to be to wire the lowest and longest branch (on the left) upwards. It was the only branch with numerous secondary branches that could be bent to become the main branch in the new crown. The rest of the tree would be debarked and converted into driftwood.

1 The Chinese juniper (*Juniperus chinensis*) was inspected from all sides to determine which areas of the tree could be converted into driftwood. A branch had to be selected to form a living crown. When the front of the juniper was selected, the following points had to be taken into account: the slight hollow in the trunk had to be visible; the new crown had to complement the driftwood trunk; and the structure of the dead trunk had to harmonize with the living part of the tree.

2 After some deliberation, it was considered safe to debark the tree from the apex down to its first branch on the left. All foliage was pruned off the branches of the trunk that were going to be debarked.

3 Every branch conforming to the Driftwood style design of the tree was debarked. Several were shortened and wrenched off to produce broken-off branch tips. A penknife was used to peel strips of bark off the trunk. The cream-colored cambium, together with other layers of plant tissue, was scraped off to expose the sapwood beneath. This layer of wood is often moist because it contains vascular cells that transport water up the tree. If carving is done immediately on this soft layer, use hand tools such as burins and gouges. If it is allowed to dry out for several months, it will turn into heartwood. This is very dry and hard so carving is easier with power tools.

4 Old scars were cleaned of debris with a router rasp. These weathered effects enhance the beauty of the driftwood.

5 Several of the juniper jins on the driftwood had to be wired and re-shaped to improve their movement and old scars were cleared of debris with a router rasp. Heavy wires were applied to the long branch to reshape it into a Slanting style bonsai, and some of the scanty branches had to be shortened to encourage back-budding. Another three years of foliage growth will be required to develop foliage clusters in the crown.

6 After final adjustments were made to the trunk movement of the living tree, the bonsai was transplanted into a shallow oval pot. Its brown, rugged surface complemented the whitened "ghost" of the juniper's former trunk. The driftwood had to be preserved by applying a solution of lime sulfur (see page 108) with a small paintbrush. Although it is better to allow the driftwood to dry beforehand, lime sulfur may be applied directly after debarking.

hollowing decay from a large trunk

In order to produce a thick-trunk bonsai for the commercial market, a deciduous tree is allowed to grow unfettered in a field for many years until the required trunk girth is obtained. The tall tree is then chopped down to a level where a small branch may be trained as the apex of a future bonsai.

In one case, a badly amputated Trident maple (*Acer buergerianum*) did not heal properly and the open wound formed a donut-shaped callus basin. The depression constantly collected water: on closer inspection, the basin was seen to contain soggy, dark-brown wood, which seemed to penetrate right down into the core of the tree. Although the tree looked quite vigorous, its future health would be threatened by rot and insects or microbes entering through the open wound. A radical solution was needed to eliminate the decay and prevent future rot.

1 With these two aims in mind, the obvious solution was to create a hollow in the trunk and a large opening running right down the stem. This would facilitate the excavation of rot from the trunk. The exact position of this opening was sketched in chalk on the trunk after selecting its front. The area was debarked with a knife.

2 A rotary cutter (specially designed for bonsai work) was used to carve out large chunks of wood and decay and grooves were gouged in the core of the tree to remove the darkened rotten wood.

3 The exposed healthy white wood was allowed to dry for several weeks, then polished with a grinder and later preserved with lime sulfur. In spring, the maple was pruned and transplanted into a bonsai pot.

4 After leaf fall, the tree was pruned again and all its main branches were wired downward. In future, the interior of the hollow must be thoroughly brushed and cleaned annually using water to remove algae, and lime sulfur must be painted on when the surface is dry. During this process, the surface of the soil should be covered to prevent spillage, as the corrosive lime sulfur might burn the roots.

improving surface roots and rejuvenating a bonsai

Beautiful surface roots are an indispensable complement to an outstanding bonsai. In addition, the root system plays an important part in the health of a tree. Because a bonsai grows in the restricted space of a pot, it must be transplanted regularly and root-pruned correctly. Renewal of the soil improves air circulation and drainage, and the pruning of old, thick roots encourages the growth of feeder roots. When these are well ramified, they encourage ramification in the crown.

1 This hawthorn was excavated from a forest about 20 years ago. It was diligently trained in pots for many years but its Informal Upright training did not reflect the elegance of its natural Broom style. In addition, its front had been selected to display the best curvature above the base of its trunk, but this had not taken into account the thick root radiating towards the viewer. This root had now become an eyesore, so it was time for an overhaul. The tree was first shortened to a level where a front branch could be encouraged to grow into a new apex. This reduction in height would enhance the girth of the base of its trunk. One plan was to transform the hawthorn into a Broom style a year later. Another plan was to correct the ugly root system and rejuvenate the tree.

2 In spring, as its buds were swelling, the hawthorn was carefully cleaned of soil and its root system neatly laid out. The conspicuous thick root was drastically shortened and the cut protected with an anti-fungal wound sealant. With its enormous root pruned, the tree lost some of its feeder roots so it had to be transplanted and rejuvenated at the same time.

3 In order to strengthen the tree's root system it needed to be planted on a mound and in perfect, well-draining soil. An upturned pot placed inside a larger pot provided the necessary mound. As the roots spread over it, this would encourage branching and thickening of the base of the trunk. Four plastic-covered wires threaded through the large pot and the upturned pot hold the tree in place.

4 Drainage gravel was placed on a layer of plastic mesh on the upturned pot and in the gap between the two pots. Then a layer of sieved Akadama (see page 156) and gravel was spread above it. The tree was transferred to the pot and fastened securely but not tightly with the four wires. Hormone rooting powder was sprinkled over the roots, especially on the amputated one, then a well-draining soil consisting of equal parts of potting soil and coarse sand was carefully worked into the root system using a chopstick. When all the roots were covered with soil, the surface was covered with moss to retain moisture.

5 The tree was watered with a solution of vitamin B1—a third of an ounce (9g) to two pints (2 litres) water—to stimulate the growth of new root cells, and was left to recover in a greenhouse for about four weeks. Notice the hawthorn's improved surface roots. It also reveals the beautiful bonsai feature of rough bark cover and an increase in the girth of the trunk. The strong, new shoots are an indication of a vigorous, healthy bonsai.

displaying bonsai

display pots

The Chinese or Japanese word bon means "tray" or "shallow pot." To fully appreciate the beauty of a bonsai it must be planted in a matching pot. The matching is determined according to a number of esthetic considerations. In general, it is important to remember that the pot must always complement and be subordinate to the tree and not compete for attention with it. Very colorful, brightly glazed pots should be avoided. Containers in discreet colors and with dull finishes harmonize better with most types of trees.

size of pot

The size of the pot should be in harmony with the dimensions of the tree. The length of the container should be about two-thirds the height of the tree. If the tree's width is greater than its height, then the length of the pot should be about two-thirds the width of the tree. If a tree has an enormous trunk girth, the depth of the container should be equal to the diameter of the trunk at its base (left). This rule is applied to all bonsai styles except the Cascade style.

TOP For bonsai with fairly thick trunks, the depth of the pot should be equal to the diameter of the base of the trunk.

ABOVE Although the length of the pot should be about two-thirds the height of the tree, if the longest branch of the bonsai could be extended outside the edge of a smaller pot, that branch would seem longer and more prominent.

The size of the pot is connected to the healthy development of the tree. Since the volume of foliage in the crown should balance that of the feeder roots in the pot, the pot must accommodate the needs of the roots. Hence, if more branching is required as the bonsai grows, the container should be slightly larger to accommodate the extra growth in the rootball. One exception must be made for the Literati style. When the rootball of one of these bonsai is squeezed into a tiny pot, there must be enough feeder roots in the small container to sustain the tree from the start. The tree must also look stable in the pot. The Literati style juniper (opposite top) was planted in a larger than normal, but quite shallow, pot to make it look balanced. Fruit trees and fast-growing trees need deeper pots because they absorb moisture faster.

shape of pot

The shape of the pot depends on the style of the tree. A Literati style bonsai is usually planted in a shallow, round pot, while forest bonsai are often in rectangular or oval pots. The character of a tree must also be considered. A powerful-looking tree, for example, will not look good in a delicate-looking container. Rectangular pots give a more formal impression than round or oval ones, so majestic trees with straight trunks should be planted in rectangular pots, while trees with curved or twisted trunks harmonize well with round or oval containers. Other factors, such as the lip of the container, its feet, any horizontal band or other ornamental detail that could complement or echo design elements in the tree, are more subjective.

matching pot to species

In general, conifers should be planted in simple, colored earthenware, unglazed pots. The color of the pot should be similar to that of the bark of the tree. Some glazes are made to match the patina of the bark. Broad-leaved trees can be matched to colored, glazed containers. The color should reflect the color of the leaves, flowers, or fruits. Pots and ceramic trays (suiban) can acquire a patina with age. To achieve this, expose them (upturned) to the elements for several years, then clean thoroughly with a soft cloth.

matching pot to posture

The length and configuration of the branches in relation to the posture of the trunk can be crucial in the selection of a harmonizing container. For example, the lower branches of an arching, windswept tree would look more dramatic if the tree were planted on a mound of earth in a shallow tray. A tree with a long first branch might be confined within the limits of the rim of the pot, or may be allowed to go beyond—a lot depends on the posture of the tree and the type of pot. In the example (opposite below) the first branch of this tropical tree from Singapore, *Baeckea frutescens*, seems longer when it extends beyond the bounds of the container. Above all, the tree should look stable in its pot. On the right, an unusual triple-trunk white pine is planted in a deep round pot at the Shanghai Botanic Gardens in China. The container allows one of the tree's sweeping branches to cascade over the rim of the pot.

materials used for pots

From a horticultural point of view, terracotta or earthenware pots are ideal because of their porosity. They allow the

BELOW The specially designed dish is slightly larger than the usual size of Literati pot but it balances the juniper's exceptional spreading crown.

BOTTOM Contrary to established rules, a triple-trunk bonsai with cascading branches looks lofty in a huge drum pot.

135

evaporation of excess moisture, but unfortunately, salt deposits often accumulate along the rim and on the surface of the pot. A terracotta pot is also more fragile and more liable to crack in frosty weather than one made of stoneware. However, stoneware is not porous, so more attention should be given to drainage. It needs large drainage holes covered with plastic mesh, on top of which there should be a layer of gravel.

Sometimes, interesting patterns are created by faults in the firing of a pot. Glazes with air bubbles or the accidental dripping of colored glaze can give a container unique features. And even if a pot is warped, that is no reason not to use it if it matches a particular bonsai.

Finally, when purchasing a pot, a simple test will indicate if it is cracked. Knock a few times on the sides of the pot with your knuckles. If you hear a high-pitched, bell-like sound, the container is fine, but if you hear a low-pitched, dull sound, it means there is a crack in the pot. Also check that the pot stands firm as sometimes one of the feet may not be perfectly level with the others.

LEFT **A selection of elegant, earthenware trays to enhance your bonsai.**

BELOW LEFT **When a Japanese maple is shaped into an elegant moyogi it should be matched with a feminine chyrsanthemum pot.**

BELOW RIGHT **A bulging oval pot was selected to reflect the hollow trunk of this field maple.**

trays and stone slabs

Although there are no rules governing the display of a rock planting in a marble tray or suiban (the Japanese equivalent, usually made of glazed stoneware,) the length of the tray should not be the same as the maximum height of the planting. Instead it should be about a third shorter or longer. The position of the planting is also important. Depending on the direction of the rock and tree, the rock planting should be placed slightly off-center.

BELOW Rock-grown bonsai can be displayed on marble trays without drainage holes. In this rock planting, a Kingsville dwarf boxwood (*Buxus microphylla* 'Kingsville') was planted in a niche (bottom right,) while two types of thyme hang precariously from cliffs.

ABOVE This suiban demonstrates how a landscape stone or suiseki is often displayed in sand or water next to a bonsai.

ABOVE LEFT A very large and shallow rock potis is a variation on a tray. This one was specially made for a Forest Bonsai of beech trees.

BELOW LEFT Forests are often planted on a natural slab of rock or on a piece of slate. This mixed forest of junipers and larches was planted on a terracotta slab.

stands

Bonsai stands come in dozens of different shapes, sizes, and designs. Traditional bonsai tables from China are often made of rosewood or blackwood. Fine bonsai tables are also produced in Japan but they are usually more expensive. The most obvious use of a bonsai stand is in the display of a Cascade style bonsai. Its pot must be positioned on top of a slightly larger square or round stand and the stand must be tall enough to ensure that a long cascading branch will not touch the ground (below right).

Other styles of bonsai are usually displayed on low rectangular tables. These must always be longer than the length of the

ABOVE **The red summer foliage of a maple is offset by its cream colored pot. It stands on a warm, reddish-brown table.**

RIGHT **A round or square cascade pot should be placed in the center of a tall stand.**

bonsai pot. Usually the table is one- or two-thirds longer than the length of the pot. A Literati bonsai has an extra-long trunk so it would look unstable on a table. Instead, enhance its elegant trunk movement by displaying it on a thin slab of wood or on a miniature bamboo raft.

In a traditional Japanese home, there is a tokonoma, or special niche built into a wall for the display of a floral arrangement or a bonsai. In such homes, people sit on the floor and look at a bonsai displayed on a table within the tokonoma. In other parts of the world, the sort of place to display a bonsai might be on top of a writing table, against a plain background, where it could be viewed from a living-room chair.

ABOVE Display area in a conventional home where bonsai could be viewed from a living-room chair.

LEFT The autumnal hues of a Japanese maple in a blue pot are matched to an ornate rosewood table.

exhibiting and viewing bonsai

viewing bonsai

The best place to view bonsai is obviously at an exhibition. Participants usually display their well-manicured trees against a plain, pale-colored background. A well-organized display will provide a description of every bonsai: name of species, style, origin (whether cultivated from seed or cutting, collected from nature, or imported from another country, and so on,) training, type of pot, and details of the owner.

Generally speaking, most bonsai growers tend to limit the height of a bonsai to less than 40 inches (1m) since larger trees must be planted in huge pots and are often very heavy.

When a bonsai is presented for viewing it must be displayed with its front towards the viewer, at eye-level, and at an appropriate distance. Unfortunately, at bonsai shows, trees are rarely displayed at the correct height for the average person.

the art of bonsai display

A bonsai should be displayed in the traditional manner accompanied by a scroll painting and an accessory. This may be an accent plant, a suiseki (see page 139) or a discreet-looking ornament, such as a tiny bronze deer or a small figure of a fisherman or some other suitable character.

ABOVE A Clump style *Acer palmatum* "Deshôjô" being exhibited at the Takagi Bonsai Museum.

RIGHT A New Zealand laburnum (on the right) with minute leaves is displayed next to an accent plant in a tiny pot.

LEFT The longest branch on this white pine points left. The bonsai should therefore be positioned on the right-hand side of the display area.

BELOW If a Cascade style bonsai points toward the right, then the accompanying scroll must be hung to the right of the tree.

The scroll painting should reflect the season or depict a landscape, or it may be replaced by calligraphy scroll with a few simple words of wisdom written on it. The accent plant may also indicate the season at which the bonsai is shown. Wild herbs, grasses, and dainty annuals that grow in the tree's natural habitat may be used to enhance the scene, while the suiseki should suggest the environment in which the bonsai species naturally grows. For example, a Cascade style juniper bonsai normally grows in rugged terrain, clinging precariously to a cliff. To highlight this dramatic feature, a suiseki with cliffs and jagged mountain peaks should be chosen to complement the display.

positioning a bonsai for display

A bonsai should not be placed exactly in the middle of a display area, but slightly off-center, depending on the direction the tree points. Thus a bonsai with a main branch pointing towards the left should be placed slightly to the right of the setting. Then the scroll should be hung on the wall to the left (above). A pine tree cascading to the right should be placed on a high table on the left, and the scroll hung on the right-hand side, with its design (in this case a fish) pointing to the left (as shown in right) towards the tree. Finally, the accessory should be placed to form a triangle with the bonsai and the scroll. This triangular composition of the three

ABOVE A bare, deciduous bonsai should be displayed with a scroll depicting a winter scene.

elements follows the traditional esthetic of Japanese garden design and in ikebana and bonsai. It reflects the ideal of asymmetric balance in a defined space.

the symbolism of a bonsai display

According to oriental philosophy, a bonsai represents mankind, the scroll signifies heaven and the accessory symbolizes earth. These three elements are selected and carefully arranged in order to suggest an environment and mood, thus a cold winter scene on the scroll and a few bamboo stems would enhance the few fruits on a leafless pomegranate (left) while other displays might feature a lone battered pine in the grandeur of a mountainous landscape, or the tranquility of meadow elms next to an accent planting of wild grasses. When we contemplate a bonsai, the tree has its life-story to tell. With special lighting effects modern displays can conjure up various moods, but this sort of paraphernalia should never be allowed to overshadow the bonsai itself.

outdoor displays

One of the best displays of bonsai is at the Chinese garden in Singapore (opposite below). Here the trees and miniature landscapes are displayed in a Chinese-style garden so they can be admired while strolling from one part of the garden to another. The collection of 3,000 trees includes all the five main styles of Chinese bonsai and an amazing assembly of locally designed tropical masterpieces. A full-time bonsai artist assisted by several gardeners tends the bonsai. It is an oasis of tranquility in the bustling metropolis.

Right in the heart of Tokyo is the Takagi Museum (see picture on page 146). Its rooftop houses a huge collection of masterpieces

ABOVE RIGHT An excellent combination of brilliant red maples is displayed next to an impressive conifer bonsai by Marc Noelanders of Belgium.

BELOW RIGHT One of the best collections of bonsai outside China is housed at the Chinese Garden in Singapore. Three thousand exquisite trees and rock Penjing [Chinese landscapes] are beautifully displayed in a splendid Chinese garden.

ABOVE Immeasurably old trees are tastefully exhibited on the roof top of the Takagi Bonsai Museum in Tokyo.

between 300 and 500 years old. Every three days, several are selected for the indoor display where they are exhibited in traditional style. The outdoor roof-garden display area can only accommodate three or five at a time. The museum also has a permanent exhibition of antique bonsai pots.

In Belgium, the noted bonsai artist, Mark Noelanders, always displays his trees very tastefully. The top photograph on page 145 shows how well the fall color combination of two varieties of Japanese maple complements the luxuriant green needles of a pine. In the foreground, wild grasses add a rustic atmosphere.

grooming a Yamadori for competition

ORIGIN OF MATERIAL: Excavated from a mountain in Northern Italy
GROOMING PERIOD: six hours

Most bonsai clubs organize events to encourage members to show their trees and share their experiences. Enthusiasts obviously make an extra effort to prepare certain trees that would otherwise be neglected. The success of a club depends on its members participating in local exhibitions or national competitions. Enthusiasts who are unsure of the standard of their trees should be persuaded to participate. It is not the winning that counts. Many of us remember our satisfaction and pride when we first dared to show our own humble bonsai at a club exhibition.

Bonsai shows are a source of inspiration for all enthusiasts and can encourage growers to improve the standard of their trees for successive shows. The *Juniperus communis* opposite was entered for competition at one of the biggest European bonsai shows a year ago. Its driftwood trunk attracted a lot of attention but the tree was not yet ready for competition, so the author was commissioned to assess it for its next competition. As a qualified bonsai judge, he was quickly able to assess the shortcomings and faults of this very impressive tree:

- No marks would be awarded for the soil surface because there was debris among lumps of unsightly moss.

- Not enough attention was given to the carving and preservation of the jins and sharis.

- Branches were badly wired and not shaped to a good design.

- The branches lacked meticulous pruning and shaping—a sign of inadequate care.

- The untidy crown was punctured with areas of improper spacing.

- The lack of a back branch meant the bonsai looked one-dimensional.

The owner of this potentially magnificent tree was given the following advice:

- To re-shape all the branches by pruning and wiring and then to allow the branches to ramify for two years to increase their mass

- For at least another two years, to hard-prune the foliage with scissors, and to finger-pinch and shape with wires.

- To scrape off some of the reddish-brown inner bark remaining on the sharis and to clean the driftwood with a router and preserve it with lime sulfur.

- To train proper back branches into visible positions from those that were awkwardly bent upwards in order to fill the back of the crown.

- Faults in the placement of branches in the crown could be camouflaged but the movement of the principal branches should be coordinated with the trunk movement.

Unfortunately, the owner preferred a quick grooming to a gradual overhaul of the juniper. Instead of the four years required to transform the tree into an outstanding example of bonsai, the author was given six hours to groom it ready for its next competition.

BELOW An excavated *Juniperus communis* with a very impressive driftwood trunk—but unfortunately it has not been refined.

1 When bark was stripped from the stem, all reddish-brown cellular tissue had to be removed. Dried-up cellular tissue can be difficult to scrape off with a knife, so a rasp was used.

2 Lime sulfur was painted on the shari with a brush.

3 Using a sharp knife to dig in, the wood was stripped off fiber by fiber.

4 A router removed shavings of wood.

5 With a burin and router, a groove was dug at the edges of the shari along the live cambium. A callus would quickly form and grow over the edge.

6 The badly wired branches had to be re-wired correctly and bent into shape to form "clouds" of foliage.

7 Even though the mass of foliage was not large, a full crown was obtained by lowering the main branches and spreading out the wired secondary branches. Finally, good-quality moss was laid on top of the leveled soil surface. The juniper won second prize at its next competition.

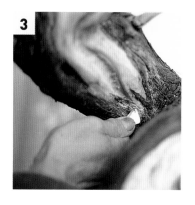

7

conclusion

I hope I have succeeded in introducing you to a better way of creating and viewing bonsai. It is how we contemplate a bonsai that enables us to understand and appreciate Zen esthetics in bonsai art. In addition to that, the contemplation of a bonsai tree is an intuitive contact with nature akin to a form of meditation. It may be for many people the best means of experiencing the special effects of Zen art.

The simplicity of Zen art, with its quiet, harmonious presentation stimulates the mind to see more than the obvious. Bonsai transcends the limitations of time and culture, communicates the artist's vision in a creative transaction that evokes a variety of sensations. Behind the creation of every bonsai masterpiece lie many years of practice, study, and patience, as well as observation of trees in nature. Our love for bonsai will eventually draw us closer to nature and the spirit of Zen Buddhism: silence, space, simplicity, harmony, compassion, humility, generosity, wisdom, and inner peace.

transplanting table

SPECIES	SEASON TO TRANSPLANT
Apple (*Malus*)	Spring, when the buds are swelling
Apricot (*Prunus* varieties)	Early spring, as soon as flowers decay
Azalea and Rhododendron	Spring, after flowering
Bougainvillea	Spring, when the buds are opening
Boxwood (*Buxus*)	Spring, when the buds are swelling
Beech (*Fagus*)	Late spring, when buds are swelling
Cedar (*Cedrus*)	Spring, when buds are swelling. Every three years
Celtis sinensis	Early spring, when buds are swelling
Cotoneaster	Spring, when buds are swelling
Cryptomeria	Spring, when the buds are about to open
Elm (*Ulmus* and *Zelkova*)	Early spring, when buds are swelling
Spindle tree (*Euonymus*)	Early spring, when buds are swelling
Fig (*Ficus*)	Spring or summer
False cypress (*Chamaecyparis*)	Spring, when buds are about to open
Gingkgo	Spring, when buds are swelling
Hawthorn (*Crataegus*)	Early spring, when buds are swelling
Hornbeam (*Carpinus*)	Spring, when buds are swelling
Juniper (*Juniperus*)	Spring, when buds are about to open
Larch (*Larix*)	Early spring, when buds are about to open
Maple (*Acer*)	Early spring, when buds are swelling
Mimosa (*Acacia*)	Spring, when the buds are swelling
Myrtle (*Myrtus*)	Spring, when buds are about to open
New Zealand Tea (*Leptospermum*)	After flowering and when new leaf buds are about to open
Orange jasmine (*Murraya*)	Spring or summer, when buds are swelling
Olive (*Olea*)	Spring, when buds are swelling
Pine (*Pinus*)	Spring, when buds are swelling
Pomegranate (*Punica*)	Spring, after the buds open
Pyracantha	Early spring, when the buds are swelling
Quince (*Chaenomeles*)	Autumn in alkaline soil
Rosemary (*Rosmarinus*)	Spring, with the appearance of new leaf buds and when flowers are decaying
Sageretia	Spring or summer
Serissa foetida	Spring, when buds are swelling
Spruce (*Picea*)	Spring, when buds are swelling
Tamarisk (*Tamarix*)	Late spring, after flowering
Thyme (*Thymus*)	Spring, when new leaf buds are swelling
Wisteria	Late spring, when flowers are decaying
Wrightia religiosa	Spring or summer, when new leaf buds are swelling
Yew (*Taxus*)	Spring, when the buds are about to open

cultivation chart

This cultivation chart shows trees and shrubs that are easy to train into bonsai. It indicates where they should be sited, in what type of soil, and when and how they should be watered, fed, pruned and wired. The chart lists the main precautions that should be

SPECIES	SITING	SOIL	WATERING
Acer palmatum Japanese maple	Shade red-leafed varieties from strong summer sun. Always site other varieties in dappled shade.	pH5.5–6. Two parts potting soil + one part grit	Keep constantly moist. Branches will be lost if soil dries out too often.
Cedrus atlantica Glauca Group Blue cedar	Full sun	pH 7. One part potting soil + two parts limestone grit	Allow soil to dry out between waterings. Spray needles on warm, dry days but not in the sun.
Cotoneaster microphyllus	Full sun	pH 5.5–6.5. One part potting soil + one part grit	Allow soil to dry out between waterings.
Crataegus monogyna and *C. oxyacantha* Hawthorn	Full sun, especially when flowering and fruiting	pH 6. Two parts potting soil + one part grit	Keep moist. Water frequently during flowering and fruiting.
Ficus religiosa and *F. retusa* Tropical fig	Full sun outdoors or on a bright windowsill indoors in winter	pH 5.6–6. Two parts potting soil + one part grit	Keep moist. Allow soil to dry out between waterings.
Juniperus chinensis Chinese juniper	Full sun	pH 5.5–6.5. One part potting soil + one part grit	Allow soil to dry out between waterings. Spray foliage on windy days.
Juniperus squamata "Meyeri"	Full sun	pH 5–6. One part potting soil + one part grit	Allow soil to dry out between waterings. Spray foliage on windy days.
Larix decidua European larch	Full sun	pH 5–6. One part potting soil + one part grit	Keep moist. Do not allow soil to dry out, even in winter.
Malus halliana and *M. floribunda* Crab apple	Full sun	pH 6. Two parts potting soil + one part grit	Keep moist. Water frequently during flowering and formation of fruits.
Pinus sylvestris Scots pine *P. mugo* Mountain pine	Full sun	pH 6. One part potting soil + two parts grit, or Akadama (see 156) only	Allow soil to dry out between waterings.
Punica granatum var. *nana* Dwarf pomegranate	Full sun, but shade from strong summer sun to prevent burning	pH 5.5–6.5. One part potting soil + one part grit, or Akadama (see page 156) only	Allow soil to dry out between waterings. Water frequently during flowering and fruiting.
Taxus baccata English yew	Full sun to semi-shade	pH 6–6.5. One part potting soil + one part grit	Allow soil to dry out between waterings.
Ulmus parvifolia (outdoors) *Zelkova schneideriana* (indoors) Chinese elm	Full sun for *Ulmus* outdoors; bright windowsill for *Zelkova* indoors in winter	pH 5–6. Two parts potting soil + one part grit	In winter, water deciduous outdoor bonsai only when soil is almost dry. Keep indoor bonsai moist as they continue to grow.

taken. In general, plants with small leaves, flowers, and fruits that regenerate after branch and root pruning are ideal for bonsai cultivation. Species of trees that produce very large leaves, such as horse chestnut (*Castanea*), or that are prone to branch dieback should be avoided. N.B. Grit is coarse or sharp sand made from crushed granite or limestone.

FEEDING	PRUNING	WIRING	PRECAUTIONS
General-purpose fertilizer	Remove adventitious buds except for those required to develop into branches.	After leaf fall and in winter; remove in spring.	Wooly aphids and scale insects. Protect from frost in winter and early spring.
Conifer fertilizer in early spring and early summer; tomato fertilizer in fall	Shorten new shoots in summer to two whorls of needles.	Any time. Branches thicken faster when trees are grown in ground.	Protect from frost. Old needles are shed every four years. Watch out for mites.
Balanced fertilizer with some bone meal	Remove suckers, but new branches can be created from adventitious buds.	Any time but check for scarring every few months	Aphids and mealy bugs. Plants infected by fireblight must be destroyed.
General-purpose fertilizer with some bone meal	Shorten shoots in summer and trim in fall.	In summer or after leaf fall	Aphids and mealy bugs. Tolerates light frost.
General-purpose fertilizer	Prune any time; shorten shoots to improve ramification and maintain crown profile.	Any time	Scale insects and sooty mould
Conifer fertilizer in early spring and early summer; tomato fertilizer in fall	Pinch off excessive growth in summer; hard and heavy prune any time.	Any time	Spray to kill scale insects, then insert systemic insecticide tablets in soil.
Conifer fertilizer in early spring and early summer; tomato fertilizer in fall	Pinch off new shoots: hard and heavy prune any time.	Any time	Spray to kill scale insects and caterpillars in webs, then insert systemic insecticide tablets in soil. Tolerates light frost.
Conifer fertilizer with some bone meal. Reduce nitrogen to retard growth in trained bonsai.	Shorten all shoots in growing season; remove adventitious buds.	Late Fall. Remove in early spring to prevent scarring.	Mealy bugs. Tolerates light frost.
General-purpose fertilizer with some bone meal. Stop feeding after flowering and before fruits swell.	Prune late fall and early spring; shorten shoots in summer.	In spring and summer	Spray to kill wooly aphids, then insert systemic insecticide tablets in soil.
Conifer fertilizer in early spring and early summer; tomato fertilizer in fall	Pinch two-thirds off elongating candles; hard prune in spring and fall; heavy prune in winter.	Late fall and winter	Scale insects. Protect rootball from severe frost.
General-purpose fertilizer with some bone meal	Cease pruning in late spring to allow flowering.	Spring to fall	Aphids and scale insects. Protect from frost.
Conifer fertilizer in early spring and early summer; tomato fertilizer in fall	Pinch out shoots in late spring; remove adventitious buds; trim in late summer.	Any time	Scale insects and spider mites. Tolerates light frost.
Scale insects and spider mites. Tolerates light frost.	Prune any time; shorten shoots to maintain crown profile.	Any time	Aphids and scale insects. Insert systemic insecticide tablets into soil when new growth emerges.

bonsai museums and parks

AUSTRALIA
Auburn Japanese Gardens
Chiswick Road, Auburn, N.S.W.
Tel: 612-98715630
E-mail: shellan@bigpond.com.au

Brisbane Botanic Gardens
The Bonsai House, Mt. Cootha Road,
Toowang, Queensland

Bonsai Koreshoff Nursery
Telfer Road, Castle Hill, Sydney, NSW
Imperial Bonsai Nursery, 18 Myoora
Road, Terry Hills, NSW,
Tel: 61-(02) 450 2455

BELGIUM
Gingko Bonsai Museum, Heirweg 190,
Laarne
Tel: (32) 93551485

Collectie Marc Noelanders,
Luchtvaartstr. 7, 3500 Hasselt
Tel: 0032-11-233499.

CANADA
Minter Gardens, 52892, Bunker Road,
Rosedale, Br. Columbia
www.minter.org

Montreal Botanical Garden, Montreal,
Quebec

CHINA
Beijing Botanical Gardens, West Hall
Tel: 86 10 62591283

Shanghai Botanic Gardens, 1100 Long
Wu Road, Shanghai
Tel: 86-21-64365523

Garden of Politics and Simplicity, Liu
Garden, Suzhou

FRANCE
Pepinerie de Bonsai-Penjing, 299,
Chemin du Val de Pome, 06410 Biot
Tel: 93 65 63

Yamadori Bonsai, 14, Rue du Collêge,
34000 Montpellier
Tel: 67 528452

GERMANY
Bonsai Museum Heidelberg,
Mannheimer Straße 401, 69123
Heidelberg
Tel: 0049 06221 84910

Bonsai Zentrum München,
Schleibheimer Straße 458, 80935
München
Tel: 089 313 1026

Bonsai Museum Seeboden, Hauptplatz
1, A-9871, Seeboden
Tel: 04762 81210

INDIA
Bonsai and Garden Landscaping,
Preyas, 3rd floor, 20, Dadyseth Rd.,
Badulnath, Mumbai 400 007

INDONESIA
Indonesian Bonsai Society, Jin.
Kembang Harum Utama, Blok C11/12,
Puri indah, Jakarta 11610
Tel: 5806642

ITALY
Crispi Bonsai Museum, Strada Statale
del Sempione 37, Parabiago, Milano
Tel: 0039-0331-554688
www.crispibonsai.it

Franchi Bonsai Museum, Via Lucchene
159, 51010 Ponte All'abate, Pescia
Tel: 0039-0572-429262.

JAPAN
Juppu-an Bonsai Museum Nagano
Omiya Bonsai Village (has at least 10
bonsai gardens owned by famous
masters:. Zuisho-en houses a fifth of
the national bonsai treasures. An
appointment is necessary to visit
these bonsai gardens.)

Takagi Bonsai Museum, 1-1, Gobancho,
Chiyoda-ku, Tokyo
Tel: 03-3221-0006

Kanuma Bonsai Park (50 miles north of
Tokyo. The Kanuma Satsuki Festival is

held in May at Kanuma City Kamoku
Center, #2086-1, Moro, Kanuma-Shi,
Tochigi-Ken 322-0026,
Tel: 0289-762310)

KOREA
Bonsai Art Park (Pun Jae Artpia), 1534
Jeo ji-Ri, hangyung-Myun, Bugcheju-
Gun, Cheju-Do
Tel: (064)72 01

MALAYSIA
Malaysian Bonsai Society, 37, Jln.
SS3/55, 47300 Petaling Jaya,
Selangor
Tel: 603 787 57911

NETHERLANDS
Bonsai Institute Terakawa
Tel: (31) 04199-6583
(By appointment only)

Bonsai Studio Chye Tan
Ryndonksestr. 3
5275 H.J. Den Dungen
Den Bosch
Tel: (31) 073-5941421
(By appointment only)

Edo Bonsai, International Trade Center
Boskoop, Belgielaan 1
Tel: (31) 01727-13755

*Hoka-en (Lodder Bonsai),
Utrechtseweg 21, Vleuten
Tel: (31) 030-6773234

PUERTO RICO
Futago Bonsai, P.O. Box 1620, Trujillo
Alto, PR 00977
Tel: (787) 755 3362

SINGAPORE
Chinese Garden, Jurong.
Tel: 65-2943455

SPAIN
Bonsai Museum Marbella, Parque
Arroyo de la Represa, Avda. del Dr.
Maiz Viñal, Marbella

Tel: 0034-952-862926.
www.sopde.es/cultura/museos/museo
20.html

Museo de Bonsai, Arroyo de la Vega,
28700, Alcobendas
Tel: 34 6570954

SWITZERLAND
Miniatur Arboretum Boswil, Chasiweg
3, 5632 Boswil
Tel: 0041 57 462420

TAIWAN
Bonsai Association, 13 Fl. No.179, Dun
Hwa South Rd. sec. 1, Taipei

THAILAND
Thai Bonsai Association, 427 Uahsuk
Soi 5, Pattanakarn Rd. Suanluang,
Bangkok 10250
Tel: 713 0590

UNITED KINGDOM
Birmingham Botanic Gardens (National
Bonsai Collection) Edgbaston
Tel: 0121 4541860

Greenwood Gardens, Ollerton Road,
Arnold, Nottingham
Tel: 0115 9205757

Herons Bonsai, Wiremill Lane,
Newchapel, Surrey
Tel: 0342 832657

UNITED STATES
Alabama: Birmingham Botanical
Gardens, 2612 Lane Park Road,
Birmingham
Tel: 205-4143950

California: Northern California Bonsai
Collection, 666 Bellevue Avenue/Lake
Merritt, Oakland, CA 94602
Tel: 510-7974727
www.gsbf-bonsai.org/collection.htm

Southern California Bonsai Collection,
Huntington Library, Art Collections and
Botanic Gardens. 11151 Oxford Road,
San Marino, CA 91108

Tel: 625-4052100
www.huntington.org

San Diego Wild Animal Park, 15500
San Pasqual Valley Road, Escondido,
CA 92027 9614
Tel: 760-7478702

District of Columbia: National
Arboretum, 3501 New York Avenue,
N.E. Washington, DC 20002-1958
Tel: 202 2452726
www.bonsai-nbf.org

Florida: Morikami Museum and
Japanese Garden, 4000 Morikami Park
Road, Delray Beach, FL 33446
Tel: 516 4950233
www.morikami.org

Illinois: Chicago Botanical Gardens,
1000 Lake Cook Road, Glenclose,
Illinois 60022
Tel: 847 8355440
www.chicagobotanic.org

Iowa: Des Moines Botanical Center,
905 East River Drive, Des Moines, IA
503162897
Tel: 515 2422934

Massachusetts: Arnold Arboretum of
Harvard University, 125 Arborway,
Jamaica Plain, MA 021303519
Tel: 617 5241718
www.aeboretum.harvard.edu/

Minnesota: Como Park Conservatory,
1325 Aida Place, Saint Paul, MN 55103
Tel: 615 4878240
www.stpaul.gov/depts/parks/conserv.
htm
New York: Brooklyn Botanical Garden,
1000 Washington Avenue, Brooklyn,
NY11225
Tel: 718 6237200

North Carolina: North Carolina
Arboretum, 100 Fredrick Law Olmsted
Way, Ashville, NC 28806-9315
Tel: 828-6652492
www.ncarboretum.org

Ohio: Franklin Park Conservatory and
Botanical Gardens, 1777 East Broad
Street, Columbus, Ohio 43203-2040
Tel: 614 6458733
www.fpconservatory.org

Krohn Conservatory, 1501 Eden Park
Drive, Cincinnati, Ohio 45202
Tel: 513 4214086
www.cinci-parks.org

Pensylvania: Longwood Gardens, Poute
1, Kennett Square, PA 19348 0501
Tel: 610 3881000
www.longwoodgardens.org

Phipps Conservatory, 1 Schenley Park,
Pittsburg, PA 15213 3830
Tel: 412 6226915
www.phipps.conservatory.org/index1.
html

Texas: Central Texas Bonsai Exhibit,
Jade Gardens, 12404 Ranch Road 12,
Wimberley, TX 78676
Tel: 512 8472514
www.wimberley-tx.com/-
bonsaijg/tree.html

Washington: Elandan Gardens Ltd.,
3050 West State Highway 16,
Bremerton, WA 98312
Tel: 360 3738260
www.kitsap.net/tour/portochard/eland
an.html

Pacific Rim Bonsai Collection,
Weyerhauser Corporate Offices,
Federal Way, WA
Tel: 206 9243153
www.weyerhauser.com/arboutus/wher
eweoperate/worldheadquarters/bonsai
collection.asp

glossary

Accent plant A small herbaceous or rock plant in a tiny container displayed next to a bonsai to complement it.

Akadama Meaning red clay balls, this volcanic soil (pH between 6.5 and 6.9) is imported from Japan. It assures the grower of perfect drainage but contains no nutrients so organic fertilizer has to be applied regularly.

Air layering A band of bark including the cambium layer is removed round a branch. The exposed area is wrapped with damp moss to encourage rooting and then completely covered with a plastic bag to prevent evaporation. When sufficient roots have formed, the branch is severed just below the tender roots and the newly rooted plant is planted in porous soil to encourage the growth of stronger roots.

Broom style An upright tree with branches spreading fan-like from the middle of the trunk, resembling an upturned broom.

Buttressing Wedge-like portions of a trunkbase which support the stem.

Callus The new bark that has grown over a wound or cut.

Cambium The layer of living tissues between the sapwood and the bark.

Canopy The peripheral foliage of a tree.

C. E. C Cationic exchange capacity is the capacity of a soil material to absorb nutrients and hold them for future use, even if the water in which the nutrients are dissolved in has evaporated.

Chasm Deep cleft or tunnel-like fissure through rock

Chi Energy force.

Clump style A bonsai with multiple trunks growing out of the ground from one root ball.

Crown Upper part of tree where branches spread out from the trunk.

Cut paste Wound sealant specially made to promote the healing of pruned areas.

Damping off A fungal disease carried in soil where it attacks seedlings.

Debark Partial removal of bark from the trunk.

Dormancy Period when a tree ceases to grow. In temperate countries deciduous trees lose their leaves and their roots are inactive.

Feeder roots Roots that absorb moisture and nutrients for the tree.

Forest Bonsai A group of trees planted in a bonsai pot simulating a forest.

Grooming Pinching or cutting off twigs and shoots with scissors to beautify the outline of the canopy of a bonsai.

Group Planting style A group of trees representing a grove.

Hair roots (see feeder roots).

Hard pruning: The cutting of lignified branches with scissors.

Ichi-no-eda The lowest, number one branch, closest to the roots of the bonsai.

Ikebana Japanese flower arranging.

Jin Preserved dead branch or driftwood.

Jinning The debarking of a whole branch.

Keto A mixture of clay and sphagnum moss.

Literati Learned person, also used as the name of a style of bonsai.

Mame Mame Bonsai are trees which are between 3 and 6 inches in height.

Mother and Child style A twin style bonsai where one trunk is distinctly smaller than the dominant trunk.

Penjing Miniature Chinese landscape.

Pensai Chinese equivalent of Japanese bonsai,

Peat moss A compacted accumulation of decayed sphagnum moss.

pH The relative acidity or alkalinity of a soil designated by its pH number, from extreme acidity to extreme alkalinity.

Pinching The shortening of a soft shoot by breaking it between the thumb and first finger.

Pine Tree style Bonsai shaped to look like pine trees depicted in classical Chinese landscape paintings.

Principal branches Major branches of a bonsai.

Potting soil Soil sold at garden centers for planting a wide range of trees and shrubs.

Raft style The individual trunks were originally large branches growing from one side of a tree. The original stem is cultivated horizontally and these branches trained to grow upwards. As soon as the horizontal stem roots, the original rootball is pruned off.

Rock pot A container made of cement or fired clay that looks like a natural piece of rock.

Sabi Japanese esthetic term describing a rustic display.

Saikei Japanese miniature landscape of trees and rocks.

Sano-eda Back branch.

Sashi-eda Longest branch of a bonsai defining the movement of the tree.

Shari Debarked areas of a tree.

Shohin An impression of movement from the trunk of the bonsai or the energy in the posture of the tree.

Soft pruning Finger pinching shoots or shortening them with a pincer.

Species Plants sharing distinctive botanical characteristics, transmitted by inbreeding.

Suiban A Japanese ceramic tray without drainage holes to display suiseki or a rock planting.

Suiseki Viewing stones in the form of mountains or other natural features, animals, etc.

Tachiagari Movement of the trunk between its base and the first branch.

Tokonoma A niche in the wall of a Japanese living room where bonsai, ikebana or objects of artistic value are displayed in traditional style.

Topping off A reduction in the height of a tree after pruning off the top portion of the stem.

Uke-da The counterbalancing branch opposite the longest branch of a bonsai.

Variety A group of plants, which in nature develop some minor differences from the species to which they belong.

Viewing stones Natural rocks (which can be held in one or two hands) with shapes suggesting mountains or other features. Usually displayed in a tray of sand or water.

Wabi Feelings of desolation, tranquility, melancholy, austerity, experienced when viewing a work of art.

Winter-hardy Capable of withstanding the effects of frost without apparent damage.

Witch's brooms Multiple branches growing from one junction of a branch.

Yamadori Tree excavated from nature.

Yugen The dramatic or mysterious impressions imparted by a piece of art.

Zen Meaning "to sit and meditate."

acknowledgments

The author wishes to thank Hoka-en in Holland, The Bonsai Shop in Holland, Gingko Bonsai in Belgium, Takagi Bonsai Museum in Japan, Jurong Gardens Pte. Ltd. in Singapore and Heron`s Bonsai in Britain for allowing him to photograph their beautiful trees.He also wishes to express his gratitude to Hotsumi Terakawa, Phach Nguyen, Ruud Lagas, Hans Rotteveel, Marc Noelanders, Leo Sleutjes, Arie Hoogenboom,Jan v.d. Westerlaken, Rien van Galen, Lim, Keow Wah, M. Suuksermsongchai, C. Sothiawanwongse, Bruno Wijman, Frank Daudt and Jos Nas.

credits

All photographs by Chye Tan except:
H. Raaymakers: pages 4&5, 20, 67, 77, 138
J. Dreryck: page 15
C. Bastings: pages 23, 142 (bottom)
D. Komen: page 110
W. v. d. Bergh: page 12l

Illustrations:
Bruno Wyman and arie Hoogenboom

Tree credits:
M. Suksermsongchai: pages 10, 40
P. Nguyen: page 11
H.Terakawa: page 12
Hoka-en: page 14
D. Use: page 15
F. Bloch: page 17
H. Rotteveel: pages 30, 91
Jurong Gardens: pages 36 (bottom), 98 (both), 145 (bottom)
Takagi Bonsai Museum: pages 37 (top), 142 (top), 143 (top), 146
C. Sothiwanwongse: page 61 (all)
P. Chan: page 90
J. v.d. Westerlaken: page 120
M. Noelanders: page 125 (top), 145 (top)
L. Sleutjes: page 128
K.W. Lim: page 134 (bottom)
R. Lagas: page 147

Word processing: Johan v.d. Berg

index